HUNGRY
FOR
WHOLENESS

Dear Mother Cora,
God bless you back a
hundred-fold for the love, mercy
& prayers that you offer His
children.

Agape, Gigi

HUNGRY FOR WHOLENESS

A Call to Pursue Healing & Restoration in
Your Father-Child Relationship

GIJI MISCHEL DENNARD
(with Robert M. Deadwyler, Sr., Posthumously)

CROSSBOOKS
PUBLISHING

CrossBooks™
A Division of LifeWay
1663 Liberty Drive
Bloomington, IN 47403
www.crossbooks.com
Phone: 1-866-879-0502

First published by CrossBooks 4/13/2012

ISBN: 978-1-4627-1514-5 (sc)
ISBN: 978-1-4627-1516-9 (hc)
ISBN: 978-1-4627-1515-2 (e)

Library of Congress Control Number: 2012905350

Printed in the United States of America

This book is printed on acid-free paper.

*Any people depicted in stock imagery provided by Thinkstock are models,
and such images are being used for illustrative purposes only.*

Certain stock imagery © Thinkstock.

*Because of the dynamic nature of the Internet, any web addresses or links contained in
this book may have changed since publication and may no longer be valid. The views
expressed in this work are solely those of the author and do not necessarily reflect the
views of the publisher, and the publisher hereby disclaims any responsibility for them.*

To the mentors, family, and friends who have inspired
and impacted my life
by their demonstration of fatherhood
as providers, protectors, defenders, teachers,
sounding boards, and comforters –
many of whom my Heavenly Father made available
in different seasons to guide me
on my own journey to wholeness –
Rev. Robert M. Deadwyler (*a.k.a. Daddy*),
Joe Johnson (*a.k.a. Fatboy*),
Dr. Norman Raiford, Father John Riley,
Pastor Chester C. Pipkin, Jr.,
Samuel F. Yette, Tim Montgomery, Dana O. Dennard,
Derrick Deadwyler, Sr., Mike O'Coffey,
Perry Fuller, and Bob Thompson.

Contents

"Sam Tucker was a stubborn man. Stubborn and bitter. When Birch and Bobby had followed their mother to the little church, it was a sort of betrayal. The embers of hatred Samuel felt against his father were fanned into a flame by his own wife and children. Everyone who lived along the road to Shiloh knew it. The twisted truth of it could not have been more obvious.

"Tonight, Birch could have stopped at any of a dozen farmhouses and been welcome. Nobody who knew the tale would have blamed him if he spent the night with his cousin J.D. and then went on home in the light of day when Samuel was more likely to be sober. But Birch had set out to go all the way home. He would sleep in his own bed tonight or out on the road. Or maybe his father would kill him when he set foot on the front porch, as he had threatened. Birch had looked death square in the face a thousand times since he left home. He wasn't afraid. He was done with fighting. His pa was alone now, with no family left but Birch. Maybe they could talk. Maybe work it out…"

In My Father's House
by Bodie Thoene

THE CRY OF FATHER HUNGER

"Look, I am sending you the prophet Elijah before the great and dreadful day of the LORD arrives. His preaching will turn the hearts of fathers to their children, and the hearts of children to their fathers."

– Malachi 4:5-6

In canvassing the treatment of the father-child relationship in post-modern literature and film from around the globe, the stories of trauma and tragedy are too numerous to count. Unfortunately, these representations of "famine" in closeness between parents and progeny hardly ever point the way to fruitful re-tilling of the ground.

It is a sad reality that "more than 75 percent of American children are at risk of paternal deprivation. Even in two-parent homes, fewer than 25 percent of young boys and girls experience an average of at least one hour a day of relatively individualized contact with their fathers."[1] Heading on a diabolical course since the early 1960s, "the United States has achieved the dubious distinction of becoming the world leader in fatherless families."[2] For too many, the day after the baby is delivered and every day that follows are filled with missed opportunities for fathers to bond with their children and influence the directions they will take in life.[3] Somehow, somewhere, we lost our understanding about the importance of fathers.

Frequently, the cycle continues. Because few men understand how their hearts have been strengthened and/or damaged by their own fathers, most do not understand the condition of their hearts as they, themselves, parent children. All men who become fathers "bring the legacy of how [they] were fathered into [their] own fathering, both for good or bad."[4]

The family was meant to be a relationship where you could learn what unconditional love was like. The home was intended to be a place where a mother and father who loved the Lord with all their hearts raised those kids up and taught the kids how to walk with God, and during that process, those kids were nurtured and accepted just as they were. They were trained up in the Word, and they were disciplined when necessary, but the home was a place where kids were supposed to feel that acceptance – "I love you because you're mine; there's nothing you can do to stop me from loving you." Then, as children got older, earthly fathers were supposed to be a representation of the Heavenly Father.[5]

All things being equal, it is always preferred that children be raised by a married mother and father. "Men and women bring diversity to parenting; each makes unique contributions to the rearing of children that can't be replicated by the other. Mothers and fathers simply are not interchangeable."[6] Both the Bible and anecdotal research clearly identify the father as the most influential person in the life of a child. "Whereas moms are priceless, irreplaceable, and needed beyond measure, they were never designed to be men or to fill the role of a dad."[7]

Fathers are the solid foundation of our life's experiences. "They are the shore we swim to when our arms and legs feel increasingly tired. They are the strength we rely on as we take our first tentative steps into the world. Dads can be tender, tough, fragile or powerful but they are probably the most uncomplicated love we will ever know."[8]

And this does not occur just in our formative years, but I remember as a young adult, finally being willing to try to learn to swim again – literally – because of my father's desire to teach me. I had been too fearful with all other instructors, including my older brother who I knew loved me. But I knew, with complete certainty – no way would Bobby Deadwyler let his baby girl drown.

Even now, as a mature adult, with my father having passed many years ago, I still find my mind wandering and wondering about what his perspectives would be on the decisions I've made in life recently – my new job, my apartment choice, how I've spent my holidays, my infrequent visits to hang out with family, and the like.

"When the Bible states that 'the glory of children is their father' (Prov. 17:6), it is revealing an important dynamic of how God has wired the hearts and minds of children." From their father, "[t]hey learn their identity . . . [t]hey learn their values . . . [t]hey learn their worth."[9]

For a daughter, Daddy is the first man she adores – the first man whose eyes shine with overwhelming amazement when he looks at her. He is the first man to fall in love with her.[10]

Having been a daddy's girl all my life, I can speak most authoritatively on the profound impact of fathers on their daughters. They shape their daughters in ways so indelible that "many women live with unwritten rules they've never thought to question." More than any other relationship, a woman's relationship with her father is "going to affect her relationships with all other males in her life, good or ill – her bosses, co-workers, subordinates, sons, husbands, brothers, pastors, college professors, and even Hollywood movie stars." Every husband either pays the price or reaps the rewards sown by his father-in-law. Dr. Kevin Leman says, "You tell me if a woman chooses Dennis Rodman over Michael Jordan, and I'll give you an accurate picture of her father!"[11]

For a son, Dad is the idol he first aspires to emulate – the mirror image of what will be and possibly the only man he will ever feel comfortable loving, until he has a son of his own.[12]

This is how Ohio-based writer Ralph Keyes expressed his hopes and expectations for a dad when he was a child:

"What I had in mind was a guy who took up more space. Someone who could hit home runs. Stare down the bad guys. Handy with a hammer, handy with his fists. At an age when bullies were picking on me, I wanted a model, someone to imitate when it came time to stick up for myself. I'd been hoping for Superman but had to settle for Clark Kent."[13]

With this backdrop, there are three basic messages in this docu-novel:

- First, all fathers and children, deep down, crave a mutually loving and trusting relationship with each other.
- Second, the role of the father is pivotal in the wholesome development of each child's identity, self-esteem, and sense of security. Whenever that role is compromised, a trail of wounds, confusion, insecurity, and distrust follows in the life of the child, one way or another.
- Third, no matter what kind of relationship you had growing up with your earthly father(s) – indifferent, horrific, or non-existent – our Heavenly Father can heal ALL the broken

places in your soul and bring you to a place of wholeness as only a perfect Father can.

There is little more satisfying than the savor of reconciliation – especially by fathers and children who have tasted bitter darkness or distance in their relationship for more than a decade. To that end, I, along with my father, and six other children, offer hope. By etching our own testimonies of restoration in this manuscript, we expect to whet that hunger for wholeness which so many still covet.

While we're sure our mothers' sides of these anecdotes are as compelling and insightful as our own, we will have to include theirs, perhaps, in another treatise. This is a narrative that expressly seeks to illustrate the heart of the fathers – from Heaven and earth – who want to be reconciled to their children, and hearts of their offspring who, in turn, yearn for their fathers' love. With insight from leading family psychologists, and parallels drawn from recorded personal experiences, we hereby attest and applaud the wonder, uniqueness, and significance of the father-child relationship. For as many as possible, we hope to give confidence to your quest for healing, forgiveness, and reunion.

GENESIS

"I am the pater familius."
—O Brother Where Art Thou?
"When I was a boy I used to dream of sailing to the end of the earth and finding my father there."
—The Voyage of the Dawn Treader
(*The Chronicles of Narnia*)

Very much like the acorn that contains all of the strength and wisdom within itself to become a great oak tree, I seem to have been born with an unswervingly confident understanding of what a "father" was supposed to be. My father's absence never diluted those expectations.

My earliest tactile remembrance of that father-hunger being satisfied was as a toddler being tickled on the floor in the living room by Fatboy – my maternal grandfather and, perhaps, the most gentle man I've ever known. In his gaze, drenched with adoration, I knew beyond a shadow of a doubt that I was cherished, that I was safe, that my every need would be provided, and that he would lay down his very life to protect me. I knew his was a love and acceptance I would never have to earn.

o Longings Deferred – Giji

My parents were wed on December 21, 1960. I was born nine months later, just 15 days before my father's September birthday. I may never know or understand all of the details surrounding my parents' separation. From my father's perspective, my mother was unable to endure through the darkness of the midnight hour to await the sunshine he was confident was coming in the morning. Whatever facts framed the metaphor, the result was that it was several months after my birth that my father held me in his arms for the first time. And it was 17 years later that the first cognitive memory of my father would be etched in my heart and mind.

For reasons that are not clear to me, and perhaps not crystal clear to my parents either, I grew up with little or no knowledge of my father. I remember missing him a lot when I was in elementary school. By the time I entered the first grade I had been taught that my legal name was "Giji Dennard." I didn't (and still don't) know why, but I was aware I would be using my mother's maiden name rather than my father's last name. On days when I was mad with my mother, or when I thought she was angry with me, I remember writing "Deadwyler" as my last name, certain that "Daddy" would be my ally if he'd been there. I don't recall my mother ever commenting about it, and I didn't know how to take that–so, eventually I stopped my not-so-subtle public outcry. But even still in junior high and high school I would sometimes find myself doodling the name "Deadwyler" during the midst of a classroom daydream.

o Left Adrift – Alex

I was just a kid when it happened – I was about five. For the most part, my dad wasn't college-educated, and he couldn't find any employment back home. So he decided to travel abroad and see if there were any opportunities for him. So the U.S. – it's the land of opportunity. It was supposed to be temporary. So my family and everyone gave him our blessing. And he left.

A couple years later he called and had a conversation with my mom sort of explaining that he wanted to get a divorce. It was kind of confusing. And she didn't really know what to make of it. We thought he went over there to find opportunities for his family. But, I guess, my parents just got separated, and we didn't really see much of him.

I can remember specifically a sense of abandonment. Because I guess as a five-year old you don't really know much of the logistics of what was done. You just know that he left. And it was like, he's not coming back. So I guess you start to question, "Why?" You start wondering if it's you . . . if it's your family. Who did what wrong? If you can try to resolve it? Yeah, just a feeling of abandonment. And as I got older, there was a little resentment, too, because there really was no explanation offered from either parent. I guess because nobody knew.

My sister, she was about three; she really grew more resentful of our father's desertion to the point where a couple of years ago she had the attitude, "I don't have a father." He would send for her to come to the States and spend some time with him and he'd take her shopping or whatever. She still wasn't receptive to the fact that she had a father.

The dad is usually there to function like a second parent; if there's one parent, there's a gap. So my mom sort of raised us alone. She didn't have the time to go to work, take us to school, pick us up from school, drop us home, drop us to sports, and still balance work and buying groceries so things would have to get cut out of the schedule. Things like extracurricular activities and sports would tend to get like the back burner. So usually when you would ask to do something like swimming or polo that involved like lessons after school and involved a time commitment she would be like, "I'm just one person; I can't do it all." So just hearing those words would kind of make you feel like, "okay, I *am* sort of disadvantaged." And I don't have this father figure to like do for me what other kids are getting.

o   Fearful Beginnings – Fran

From as early as I can remember, my father always drank heavily, so my earliest recollection of my father was one that was not very pleasant. I can recall his calling our house and I'm on the phone and he was like yelling at me. I was paralyzed with fear at the sound of my father's voice. And that would somewhat set him off a little bit. So he would follow that with, "Do you hear me talkin' to you?" And I would just cry. My mother actually had to tell me this part, but I was just standing there with the phone to my ear and tears streaming down my face saying nothing. Then she took the phone and heard him saying, "Don't you hear me talking to you?" Even when I went to visit my father, I would just cry at the sight of him; whenever he got near me, I would just cry. So those are kinda' the earliest recollections—when I was approximately six years old.

We didn't live too far from each other. Milwaukee's kind of a small town. The area where the Black community lived wasn't that large, so we probably lived not more than a mile and a half or so from where my father lived most of my life.

He still lived with my grandmother—his mother—and I had aunts who also lived at the house. What would happen is my oldest aunt, who is younger than he, is the one who would always come pick me up. Really, she was bringing me to visit her and the family. Of course my dad would be included, but he wasn't there a lot of the time. So whenever he would come home, I would become withdrawn, quiet and cry, but he wasn't there a lot.

As I grew older and got out of that stage of being so emotional, eventually I stopped crying every time I saw him, and started having some kind of regular conversation and contact. Granted, he would show some positive affection sometimes. He would buy me gifts. I remember he bought me a bike– my first bike—and a camera, when I was younger. So I do recall the times we could be cordial but still, he was not usually at the house a whole lot when I would go over to visit his side of the family.

My mother did positively encourage the relationship. And actually on holidays, like Christmas and Easter, she would usually take me by his mom's house – and his house – to visit. I think that was one of the things that helped me come out of it; when my mother was there, I was pretty cool. I stayed sheltered under her quite a bit. It helped me to relax in my father's presence when she was around.

o Intermittence – Felecia

I am 53 years old now, and my first memory of my father is from age two. He was always very gentle, loving, and attentive. He only whipped me once in my life. I was about three. That was the most hurtful thing ever. But then he immediately hugged me and kissed me afterwards.

My dad and my mom split up when I was two. I don't remember seeing much of him until I was about five, and I believe it was because he was in the military. My parents married very young–they were both teenagers. In those days, you didn't have children out of wedlock, so they got married. From that separation there was an estrangement, but there was contact with my grandmother from my father's side, and I found that we spent more time with my maternal grandparent and family members than my father's family for whatever reason. But I do remember being close to my grandmother on my father's side – spending weekends with her, that kind of thing.

After my parents split, for a while, we lived in an apartment. I believe we ended up back at my grandparents' because my mother found it hard to make ends meet. Later on she told me that because she was so young – she was 16 when they married – she didn't know anything. My grandmother did everything – she did the cooking, the washing, the ironing, and my mom and my aunt, they didn't do house chores and that kind of thing. It was a very strong Christian home, so we ended up back with my grandparents and I just loved that; I loved my Nana and Papa. They were my world. And, I guess because of the distance or the feelings between my two parents, there wasn't much contact. It was a very limited, on-again, off-again, kind of thing.

I'm a person who always has adapted to change really, really quickly. I think it was because change was so very prevalent in my childhood. I think changes and shifts would occur at the drop of a hat; you had to adapt. If you didn't, then it would be a problem.

I was always glad to see my father and he was always glad to see me, but I think because of my mom's and dad's relationship, he would just as soon not go there and not deal with it because there was some resistance on my mother's part. I believe she was holding out hope that something would happen and they would get back together. It was a first love kind of thing. And when that didn't happen, they just went their separate ways.

I was the first in a series of firsts. Both my parents had been virgins prior to my arrival. Now when I was two, there was a second baby, and he died from SIDS at six months old. That was the turning point in their marriage. I learned through talking to my dad, as an adult, that he was the kind of person who didn't let stuff go. His long-term memory was very, very sharp. Short-term was a different story. But things from 40 and 50 years ago in his life . . . he was sharp.

He confided that he thought that there was something more that my mom could have done to prevent my brother's death. Even though there's all of this literature now about SIDS and nobody knows why it happens, and so forth–in his 19-year-old mind, he was saying, it's her fault. So I think that played a part in his drinking to a degree. And I think he was probably borderline because I think he was 19 or 20 when he went into the war. When he came home, he was a different person.

o Love Imprisoned – Kellee

My parents were divorced before my father got locked up, but I was probably like four or five when they actually divorced. I don't really remember that time-frame too well. But I was about nine when my dad went to jail. So that was really the beginning of the separation. Because even though my parents were divorced, he was still around. We still did things as father-daughter, and he was always a good father. But it wasn't until he was actually incarcerated for 10 years when our relationship – although good – was still strained because he wasn't at home; he wasn't readily accessible.

I have a half-brother and a half-sister. I don't think I've ever met my sister. I've tried to reach out to contact her a couple of times throughout the years, but she and her mother just want to be separate and kinda' do their own thing, and they don't really want to be bothered with my father, nor me and my brother, because her mother had other children, so she just had those siblings.

My dad is an artist. I remember he always drew nice pictures for my birthday. One day my dad, my brother, and I, along with his girlfriend (at the time) and her family, went to the Bronx Zoo. What started out as a fun-filled day, ended with tears. My brother accidentally hurt my father's girlfriend's son's foot and my brother was spanked more harshly than I felt he deserved. Since that day, I never liked my dad's girlfriend or her family. So I used to always want my dad to get away from her, but he's married to her now.

My half-brother and I grew apart. We were around each other when we were little, but as time went on and when my dad went to jail, that's when we really became separate. We didn't really connect again until I was 17 or 18, and we're about four years apart. We talk now and we have access to each other, but we don't talk that much. He's in his own world. In his mind, he feels sometimes that the family separated themselves from him, but it's really him who's separating himself from us. He's choosing to stay in a homosexual life-style and because of that he's just doing his own thing, with his own life and whoever he's dating at the moment. He'll send me a birthday text and stuff like that but we don't really talk that much. He'll say, "Oh, I'm coming to Virginia to come see you," and then I'll never hear from him. Or he'll actually be in the same state as me and won't even call or text and I'll have to find out on Facebook that he was in town. We're not as close as we were when I was living in New York and doing some of the same things as he does. We really got separated once I became saved and started trying to live a godly life.

*   *   *   *   *

But there are other ways for a father to be absent from his family. "Being fatherless does not just mean losing a father through death, divorce, or illegitimate birth." According to research by Dr. Ken Canfield, one survey of more than 1,600 adult men revealed that "more than 50% said their fathers were emotionally absent when they were growing up."[1]

Samuel Osherson, author of *Finding Our Fathers*, asserts, "There is a deep hunger on the part of men to feel that they're valued and appreciated and beloved by their fathers." Unfortunately, he notes, sons frequently wind up perplexed about their relationships with their dads. "Their fathers work very hard, they sacrifice, but they're not present."[2]

o   Painful Presence – Isaiah

1964 was a pivotal year for us as a family. My father, when he came to California, actually wanted to go to law school and become a lawyer. However, with the beginning of his family, he couldn't do that; he had to support his family. So, he had several jobs and the job he had before 1964 was as an L.A. County Sheriff. Although my dad had the title of Sheriff, he was riding around town slumped in his seat, with his eyelids right below the window, so he couldn't see anything. He wasn't trying to be a crime-fighter. He wasn't a guy big on power. Actually the reason he became a Sheriff was because he kept getting too many speeding tickets and he figured "if I can't beat 'em, join 'em."

So in 1964, my dad was at the Rose Bowl and he was doing extra duty as a Sheriff, and a man came up to him and asked him if would he like to have a job working in insurance. My dad said, "Sure." So he went down and got hired as a claims adjuster for All-State. That year, our family moved from almost in Watts to a multi-racial community, which later became known as South Central L.A. Another thing happened to my father, as well, in '64, he became involved with the NAACP, and he got elected Secretary of the Los Angeles branch.

Now, prior to this, my father would come home from work, and he'd spend time with me and my brother and my sister. We'd play ball and do different things and have fun. And at that time, I really looked up to my father as my hero and role model.

I'll never forget we had come home from church on Sunday, and I had a football in my hand, and I said, "Hey Daddy, you want to go outside and throw the football?"

And he said, "No, I have an NAACP meeting."

And I said, "Not that again."

And he got very angry and said, "Don't you ever say that again." He started really yelling and screaming. When it happened, I remember going to put the football down, and then I went and laid on my bed and cried for like two hours. And the feeling could never leave. That's when stuff got bad.

It got worse as things went on. My father, to his credit, was not raised with his father. My grandfather abandoned my father when he was about the age of one or two years old. There're two stories. Either he had another woman on the side or he was beating my grandmother while she was pregnant with my dad's younger brother. At the time, there was only my aunt and my dad and then his younger brother. Or, he came home one night at 11 in Vicksburg, MS, in 1933, and so Big Momma hit him over the head with a skillet. And my grandfather, we think for spite, took my aunt and my dad away from my grandmother and gave them to his mother and his grandmother and said, "Here. Raise these kids."

So I grew up very insecure. And it got worse as I got older. My father for some reason—maybe because I'm the first-born– seemed to have had his own personal mission to live his life through me. When I didn't meet his expectations, he would lash out at me. There were three incidents, in particular, that I never forgot. By the time I got to be in high school, I just hated him, which is one of the reasons why I went to Howard; I wanted to be as far away as humanly possible from my father.

The first incident occurred, I think, when I was about eight or nine years old. My brother and I were in the Cub Scouts, and they had what they call a "Jamboree." And what they'd do is go to a local area, like a big park, and they would set up all these booths and every den would have to come and represent what they did, work with models, and stuff like that. Well, I really wasn't good with my hands. So what I did was go around to other booths, met all these other boy scouts, and hung out with them. At the end of the day, I hadn't done a whole lot, but I really had a good time. So my brother stayed in the booth and he made all this stuff; my brother was good with his hands. And my father started berating me in front of my family telling me how he was ashamed to have me as a child, how that I was a failure, and I remember sitting in the back of the car and I just started crying. My mother said, "Hugh, stop it! You're hurting his feelings." He screamed, "He needs his feelings hurt!" And he railed on me all the way home.

The second thing that stood out was a day I was out playing in the back yard—I was only about 11 years old. Suddenly my dad—I don't know what happened—started to chase me in the back yard. And when he started chasing me, I started running. As my father got closer and closer, I looked back and there was a strange look on his face, so I started screaming for my mom.

"Don't call your mother!" He chased me all around the backyard; tears were running down my face and I was just screaming out in fear.

My mother said, "Hugh, you're scaring him!"

"He needs to be scared!"

Finally, I ran inside. My mother stood between me and my father. And she said, "Hugh, he's had enough."

My dad said, "Well, he needs to toughen up" and all this kind of stuff. That took me about a week to recover from. I never knew what he was going to do.

But I still wanted his approval. I still wanted to be the kid he would take out in the backyard and play football with. I think the last time I tried to get his approval– before I started being indifferent—I was 13, and they had a father-son day at our junior high school. My dad came and I was so excited he was there, but he was very cold, he was aloof, he kept his hands in his pockets, and remained very distant. We had a little meal there and during the meal he said very little and seemed like he wanted to go. When I saw what all the other boys had with their dads, I realized this is not what I wanted. So we went home and I felt like, I really don't matter to him at all. Within a couple of years—by the time I was 15—I just hated him. I hated coming home. I hated talking to him. And I really didn't want to have anything to do with him.

There was another incident that happened when I was in adolescence. When you got into the 7th grade, you could join the youth choir at our church. I played the trumpet so I could read music—treble clef, anyway—I wasn't the greatest singer, and my family is a singing family, although most of them can't carry a tune in a bucket. They really can't sing, but they like playing the piano and doing these musical things. I basically hated it.

So I was out playing with some of my friends, my dad called me in and wanted me to sing this part on the piano. We had a baby grand piano in our home. He started playing the notes and I just kinda' sang, I thought it was just a song, and my dad got really angry and said, "How dare you sing like that! You better get in there and sing it right!"

I'm thinking, "What are you talking about?" And I didn't realize that when you sang, the notes on the scale were the notes you were supposed to sing – I knew it playing the trumpet, but I was thinking "What is he talking about?" And I tried again. It was a piece of music I wasn't that familiar with. My dad had me standing up there for almost 45 minutes trying to sing three measures. We went over it and over it again. By the time he got through, tears were running down from my eyes.

And he said, "If that's the best you can do, you don't need to be in any youth choir!"

I said, "Well, Dad maybe I need to stop singing."

And he said, "Yeah, you need to stop. You're an embarrassment." My mother intervened, but once, again, my day was ruined.

By the time I was a young adult and out on my own, I didn't care how he felt. I didn't care what he thought. And I didn't want to have anything to do with him. I'd call the house and talk to my mom, he'd answer the phone and I'd say, "Hey, Dad, it's Isaiah; let me speak to Mom." He'd pause and he'd give the phone to my mother. And he was wondering why I had nothing to say to him.

FACES & PHASES OF MY FATHER

Desperate stubby fingers pushing pictures 'neath the door
And longing to be listened to, by the man that I adored
Inside someone who needed me just as much as I did him
Still unable to unlock the door that stayed closed inside
of him

                            – Michael Card, "Underneath the Door"

o   Scribbles on Blank Pages – Giji

Periodically my mother would say things like, "You giggle just like your father when you do that," like when putting on cold roll-on deodorant in the morning. And she occasionally told funny stories about him, like the first time he went crabbing and ran out into the school of crabs with the net to catch the scurrying victims. But those conversations were few and far between. I always felt awkward at those moments anyway because I wasn't sure if the memories of my father brought my mother pleasure or pain, and I was afraid to ask. Otherwise, my mother rarely discussed my father, their marriage, the circumstances of my birth, or any "related" subjects.

One day, somewhere around the age of ten, I asked my mother what I thought was some random, innocent question about my father. For reasons that neither she nor I can remember, her response to me seemed caustic and uninviting. I silently vowed that day never to bring "him" up again. But that did not quench a lurking curiosity.

In the meantime, a very significant father figure entered the picture who would remain a noteworthy thread in my father fabric. You know kids can always spot insincerity. So of all the men playing suitor to my single mother – Mr. Russell, Mr. Reeves, Mr. Jackson, the one I called "Romeo," – only one of them was also genuinely interested in ME, personally: Mr. Nelson Ripley. Aside from his frequent visits to our house and his "dates" with my mom, he orchestrated our own special times–when we'd go buy these huge bags of dog food for my Belgian shepherd, Shane, or where he'd take me down to the wharf to buy my favorite fish, red snapper, and try to teach me how to eat raw conch with hot sauce [that lesson never got received well]. He would listen with interest about my academic challenges and achievements, my silly pet experiences, and even my struggles in communicating with my mother.

About three years into my very comfortable relationship with Mr. Ripley, I was introduced to my first official "spiritual father." Father Riley planted and watered seeds which sprouted a whole new concept: a personal relationship with Jesus. It was in confirmation classes that I began to learn the privileges and responsibilities which accompanied joining the family of God. It was short-lived, however, because we moved away a year later.

Then came that fateful day outside our apartment in Tampa, Florida where Mr. Ripley crossed the line: he called me his "daughter." A wave of fear and resentment overcame me. Despite the appreciation I had for his attentiveness and investment, as far as I was concerned he had no right to call me that. I was 13 and really didn't understand why I felt that way. It wasn't until I got to college, when challenged to write a paper in class, that I discovered the problem. As the title of the paper indicated, my father's shoes were "Too Empty to Fill." In my puerile mind, if I accepted this man as my father, that would somehow thwart any hope of my ever knowing my REAL father . . . or so I thought.

o Sporadic Visits – Alex

I did go up to meet my dad a couple of times. I think the first was around age 11 or 12. I went to the States. Met him. I think my mom went with me, too, so we stayed at his place. My sister went also. It was cool. It was sort of diplomatic in a kind of way. It wasn't really like a reconnection or a bonding, per se. We just spent some time, like he took us shopping. He's a good cook so he cooked a lot. His food is awesome. I guess that was the extent of it. It was more focused on exploring the States and New York, as opposed to like spending time with him. And in any case, he was always working too. So whenever we did go over – up to this day – we really don't spend that much time with each other. He's usually working . . . which he has to do; it's not even optional.

During the time that I was beginning to build a relationship with my dad – ages 16 to 19– my sister was still very resentful. And as much as I would try and get her to come around, it just didn't work. Even to this day, my dad and my sister have a more "conditional" relationship. As long as he continues to provide for her whatever she needs to get, then she will acknowledge that he's her dad.

My dad remarried later on, so he has more kids now. So we have other brothers and sisters. If an instance arises where my sister can't get what she needs – even if he really can't provide it, which is often the case, the first reaction that she will have is, "Oh. Well you take care of these other kids, but you don't take care of me." So there's still that resentment there. When I look at him now, I know he's a really good example of a man who does what he needs to take care of his family.

o   Deeper Waters – Fran

I had encouraged my father so much during the time we had reconciled – during the times that he felt low. He felt I was the person he wanted to confide in; I encouraged him about a lot of things that he would beat himself up about. And I would help him not condemn himself about a lot of things. We had a lot of heart-to-hearts about things I never imagined I'd have conversations with him about – mainly about some things in his life that he wasn't happy with. We talked about the drinking, talked about how he'd tried to quit a lot of times and he admitted he felt like he just couldn't quit. It gave me a great deal of peace to know that he and I had reconciled before he passed, that he knew I loved him, and that I knew how much he loved me. It was all out. And even though the relationship was not as close as I had hoped it would be – I had visions of our being even closer – I still had no regrets about where our relationship was at the time he passed.

o   Puzzle Pieces – Giji

During a visit to Auntie Barbara (my mother's sister) and Uncle Jimmy's house in 1977, I had the experience of talking with my father's father for the first time. It came about when I suddenly blurted out, "I always wanted a brother named Ricky and a brother named Mickey." As though she had seen a ghost, my aunt hesitatingly informed me that I **did** have a brother named Ricky and a sister they called Mickie. And in that bizarre moment, my aunt decided to defy my mother's wishes, began to whittle away the wall of separation, and introduced me to my father's family.

Uncle Jimmy and my father are first cousins and were reared together in Wilmington, Delaware. Their son, Jan, just a year-and-a-half my junior, had somewhat regular communication with our paternal grandfather. Through subsequent periodic conversations with Daddy Ed, and with Uncle Jimmy and Auntie Barbara, I found out a number of interesting fragments about my dad: he had been married before he married my mother (from which came my brother Rick, and my sisters Carol Ann, Mickey, and Terri); at some point he had been involved with drugs and in prison; he had been quite a ladies' man and an athlete, including a boxer, in his younger days; he and my mother had met at his grandmother's funeral; he was now an ordained minister (I knew he had been when he and my mother got married); he was remarried (from whence came my younger brothers Ross and Bobby) and might be living in Atlanta or Pennsylvania; and I was probably a honeymoon baby.

These bits and pieces of my father's picture puzzle only fueled the flames of my desire to find him. So, despite the fact that by then I thought that asking my mom questions about my father was "taboo," I somehow mustered the courage to ask her if she minded if I invited my father to my graduation from high school; it had been at least five years since I had mentioned him at all. Yet, I am not sure which made me more nervous–the prospect of asking Mommie or the cool, casual response I got from her once the question was out there: "I don't care . . . if you can find him."

Obviously I had pondered braving this request prior to actually asking because I already had developed a strategy for getting an invitation to my father although I had no idea where he lived. I figured I would just mail it to Daddy Ed's address and he'd send it to my dad. Despite the fact that they were not on good terms, of which I was not aware at the time, my grandfather did do as I had hoped and forwarded the high school invitation addressed to Rev. Robert M. Deadwyler–*a.k.a.*, my father.

○ Second Sets – Felecia

My father started a new life and my mother started her new life and that's what happens when you have kids—kids are in the middle, especially when the parents don't have an agreement or a meeting of the minds in terms of what's going to be the upbringing of the child or children.

So my father went on to re-marry and there's another set of children with his second wife. And then my mother had more children with other people. So I'm the oldest of both sets of children.

I didn't feel any resentment or anything like that, I was just open. Because, again, I would see him. And I knew that seeing him was precious. So I would make that last . . . because I didn't know when I would see him again.

He didn't come to my high school graduation. He didn't come to my 6th grade graduation. He didn't come to my 9th grade graduation. But for him, it was a big deal. For me, the day of graduation he wasn't there, it was a big deal. The day after graduation, it wasn't a big deal—I was over it. He held onto the "I shoulda' been there" and the guilt; I don't do that.

Now, I remember when there came a time that he introduced me to who was going to be my step-mom. I always called him by his name – Jerome. I never called him "Dad" or "Daddy" or "Father," or anything like that. That was the kind of relationship we had. And I noticed that there was a difference between my relationship with him and the relationship with him and his other children with his second wife. They answered him, "Sir." And when he said, "Jump!" they said, "How high?" And when I called him by name, they would look at me like, "ooohhh, you gon' get it!" And it wasn't that way.

I've come to know as I've gotten older that part of that, I perceive, was his guilt for not being there. He allowed me latitude that the other two didn't get. I drove his car; nobody touched his car –ever. And when they saw me pull up in the driveway, it ended up causing a divisiveness on their part towards me. I didn't realize for a long, long time, where that was coming from. But really, at that point, I didn't really care. My thought was at least you had him. And he was there every day of their lives. They never wanted for him. And they never had to wonder where he was. There were times when we lived maybe 30 minutes apart and didn't know where the other one was for many, many years.

I've learned that part of my estrangement from my brother of my father's second marriage, first, has to do with his seeing me treated very differently by our father than he was. Secondly, they grew up hearing, "The only time we hear from you is when you need something." So now they kinda' pull away because they think when I initiate contact or when I try to talk to them, it's because I want something, rather than making the connection and staying in touch. I don't have a hidden agenda in terms of wanting stay connected to them, but I can't do anything about that. But I understand that's the source of the distance. In those days, people didn't do what they do now in terms of going after you for child support in court and divorce and all that kind of stuff. My father wasn't very forthcoming as far as that was concerned.

My father was the law in his house, which extended years later to my daughters as they visited with their grandfather. No one ever questioned it saying, "When are those kids going back home?" Nobody ever said a word. Those are Jerome's grandbabies and they're going to stay here for as long as he says it's okay – even for a two-month stint once. I called him and said, "Ok. You can bring 'em home now." I'd had me some fun and a nice break. Everything was alright.

o Emotionally Bankrupt – Isaiah

So my dad had a couple of stigmas growing up. The first was, he was from a broken family. And in the '30s, especially in the South, that was really frowned upon. The other thing that happened was my dad's great-grandmother loved boys, but my dad's grandmother loved girls. When my dad's great-grand-mother died and my dad's grandmother was raising my aunt and him, she despised my father. She really abused him emotionally. The grandmother decided to move, so she had my father pack all of her belongings and all of my aunt's belongings and move them to another house in Vicksburg. Well, my dad went to go pack his stuff and she said, "Oh you don't need to pack that; you're not coming with us." So he was abandoned at the age of eight years old during the Depression.

I couldn't get my dad to talk about it, but as I talked to his brothers and sisters, they filled me in on what really happened. So my dad, really, was living in a shack, without a floor, living on some dirt; it had no heat, no running water. And he would miss school to go caddy on a golf course or set-up pins in a bowling alley. And as recently as about

2004, my dad and I were talking, it was an overcast day and my dad said, "You know, it wasn't until 1966 that I didn't get depressed when I saw an overcast day." I was like, "Well, Dad, why was that?" He said, "Because if it rained, I couldn't carry a bag that day, which meant I couldn't eat that day."

My dad also was mocked and ridiculed all the time. They used to call my dad "pee boy" because my dad only had one set of clothes. And he would be so nervous about the next day, he would urinate on himself in the bed. Because he had nothing to change into he went to work smelling like urine. So that was one thing that really cut him down.

Then my grandfather finally invited my dad to come live with him—by this time, my dad was 16 years old—and my grandfather had moved to Alabama and had married another woman. My aunt told me that when my dad got off the train she said my dad's sleeves on his jacket came a little below his elbows and that the pants he had were right at his calves. When she asked, "Why are you wearing this suit?" my dad said, "This is the best suit I have." So he was ridiculed and mocked and rejected most of his life, and during the formative years of his life.

The Civil Rights Movement was in full swing in 1964, and for one of the first times in my dad's life he had a position in life that commanded some respect. So part of what was going on, which I couldn't understand as an 8-year-old, was that this was the first time my dad was able to hold his head high. He wore a suit when he went to work. He was driving a late model car. He was doing things that had some legal aspects. So for him, part of what was going on in his life, it was his first time to feel like he had value. And the NAACP meant a lot to him. While he was doing it for us, I just wanted my father. I didn't care about all of that; I wasn't thinking like that.

To my father's credit, he was an excellent provider. He was an excellent role model in terms of taking his family to church. Of always dressing a certain way. His vocabulary was large. He was involved from a financial standpoint with our family. I never had to wonder if the lights were going to be on or food in the refrigerator or was I going to go to college. All those things were givens.

It's taken me years to reconcile the issue that my father was not equipped emotionally to be a father. He was equipped to provide finances for the family. He wasn't prepared emotionally to give and to share and to be open and to be vulnerable and to be accessible. He was light years better than his father, but because he was emotionally bankrupt, as a result, as kids, we all kinda' caught it. What he never had, he couldn't give us.

My brother and I were talking at a time he was going through a divorce with his first wife, and Brent said, "You know, Isaiah, it's kinda' scary that we can cut off our emotions and keep moving as if nothing's happening."

And I said, "Well, Brent, you had to be able to do that in our household if you wanted to survive."

And he said, "Yeah; that's kinda' sad isn't it."

So we learned at an early age: don't feel anything – just move. If you feel something, you're not going to survive emotionally. You gotta' tow the line, do what you're told to do, don't make any trouble, and you might be okay. So it was kind of a tough thing.

And even though we resolved our differences, he never knew how I really felt. I didn't feel like it was going to be profitable to bring those things up – or important to bring those issues up – because what's done is done. You can't go back and change it. And now that I understand more about him, I've had more compassion. But it did not change the hurt that I felt.

Another thing he'd do all the time is he'd compare my brother to me. He'd talk about how great my brother was – my younger brother. And my younger brother has his name, by the way. I found that I was kind of a throw-away kid. He did that even after our relationship got on better footing.

○ Headline News – Kellee

Because it was such a high profile case, it was all over the news, talk show hosts always had something to say, and then, going to school, people used to make fun of me and say things like "choo-choo." My father was a train conductor for the New York City Transit. He was a heavy alcoholic. He had been up all night drinking the night before, up to a couple of hours before his shift was about to start. Even though he says he wasn't necessarily "drunk," his alcohol content was twice the normal limit. Plus it was really hot in the train. So he had passed out, the train jumped over some tracks; five people died and over 200 were injured.

So since my father's trial was so widely publicized, I was scared to talk about it when I was younger. When people would say things like, "choo-choo," I always was ready to fight in my father's defense. Or if someone tried to make fun of me, I would be embarrassed and scared to talk about it because I never wanted to run into anybody who was part of a family where someone had passed away. I was always scared of that. Therefore, I just kept it to myself.

For the most part, I missed him. I missed having him around. I remember just crying when I was watching "Geraldo" – back in the day – and Geraldo had said something that I didn't like about my father's case.

I remember the day it happened, my mom was watching the TV and she just freaked out. She wasn't sure what to do, so the first thing she thought of was to call the doctor's office and make me an appointment. I remember being at the doctor's office and she was making phone calls. I knew something was wrong, but I didn't know what. She never told me the details. It was like: "Ok, Daddy wrecked a train. Some people died. And Daddy's going to go away for a long time." She never went to any of the trials. My mom didn't tell me because I was too young to be able to handle what all was going on.

My life period, was severely impacted by this forced separation . . . I don't want to blame it all on my dad for his not being there, but if he were around – his physical presence– I would have been able to know better my worth as a woman, instead of trying to figure that out by dating or trying to find validation through sex.

Not too long ago I actually sat down and started going over 10 years of letters – I organized and put all the letters that my dad ever wrote to me, sorted by year and month – I realized through the letters, he had things in there about sex and being pure and all these scriptures about being good and "I love you." So he was there, advising me through my teen years, but I wasn't saved and it wasn't sinking in. But now that I'm an adult and I'm saved, I know now, having re-read all the letters, I felt so stupid when I realized he actually was there, but I wasn't smart enough or educated enough or emotionally or spiritually mature enough to receive it.

Another thing about my dad and his brother is that they're very needy people; they kinda' need a woman. They can't really think or function that much on their own without a woman. Without a woman, they're more into alcohol and drugs. That part I always knew about my father and I didn't like that part—I didn't understand why he'd have this woman who was treating him like crap.

Of course, as a child, I wanted my parents to get back together for the longest time. It wasn't until I was an adult that I could see why my mom wasn't so inclined to jump right into it – because he wasn't able to make decisions. It was always like, "O.k., Honey, whatever you say; whatever you want." Or if he gets frustrated he goes out drinking.

The drinking part, I really didn't know about. I would hear about it, but at nine, I hadn't really seen it for myself. And I didn't see that kind of stuff until about three years ago when he actually came to live with us for a little while. And that really upset me terribly because he had gotten drunk to the point where he had fallen out somewhere and the hospital was calling me to come get him with alcohol poisoning. That was the first time I'd ever seen him like that. And it just hurt me so bad. He still struggles with it. And he's always been in and out of programs. That's the part that I don't care for—the fact that he just can't get it together, I guess.

I know that part of that is because of his childhood, having a father who wasn't really a father. The man who I always thought was my grandfather is not because, to this day, my father does not know who his real father is. My grandmother—back in the day—whenever her husband would leave for sea, she slept with whomever. She never told my father who his dad was. And when he would ask, they would get in a fight. If one of his brothers were there, he would start defending Grandma and the brothers would start fighting. So I don't know who my grandfather is—the real one. So it's that generational curse type stuff. Because he went through that, that didn't really give him all the male characteristics he should have had.

o One Drink Too Many – Felecia

My father did drink, but not to the point that he wasn't functional. He was what I would term a functional alcoholic. Alcoholics who get up and go to work every day, don't call out, they're never late, but they do what they do after hours.

On one occasion I witnessed a full-blown episode. For many, many years, I worked in a carry out. It was a blast! I worked there on weekends. And that was a means for me to get my school clothes during the summer—put them in lay-away, pay on them, and when school hit I had my shoes and everything else. It's not that that kind of job paid a lot of money, but tips were good.

On Friday nights and Saturday nights, we were open until 4am. And my shift—although I was underage to work and was supposed to be home in the bed sleep—was 8pm to 4am. Around 2 or 3am, when the clubs closed, and the people were pretty inebriated, they want something to eat, and we were one of the few places that were still open. You might not be able to get anything on the grill, but you could get a rib sandwich and some potato salad; we had some good food. And my father came in . . . and he was ripped! At that particular point, my mom was working there too; she was the one who got me the job. He walked in and ordered. I spoke to him by name. I was 18 and had not seen him in six years, but even though I looked just like him, he had no idea who I was. My mom inquired, "You don't know who THAT is?" He said, "Aw, I think I know her from somewhere."

So he was in there a little too long, I think, for what he was getting, so his wife came in to see what was taking him so long. They didn't know my mother and I worked there. Since his second wife and my mother could not stand to be in the same room or the same place at the same time, my mom did the right thing, and removed herself from whatever she was doing with her customer, and made herself invisible. When his wife realized that he didn't know who I was, she took him back to the car and she came back in, embarrassed and apologetic. My attitude was, "Whatever. Drunks come here all night. It is not a big deal."

I've never been one that falls apart over stuff; it's not in my make-up. If and when I do, it's drastic—it's bad and people want to call somebody for help when I fall apart. So that's why I don't, cause it's either way up here, or not at all. And that's why I'm the go-to person in the family because they know that I'll have a clear head to get through a thing.

The next day, I thought it was hilarious. To me it was a big joke because I knew that's not where his heart was. Even though I knew that, it really hurt him, and he carried that to the day he died. As much as I forgave him, the more he internalized the guilt about it. I tried to encourage him, "Get over it. I have." It's not even anything that would be unforgiveable; I'm grateful just to be able to talk with you now. By then I was thirty-something. But there was something about him that just would not let go; he just couldn't.

My father knew the Lord, grew up in church, but I think as he grew older and experienced war, I think that changed. He was different when he came home; he drank when he came home. And he never really talked about it much; he was a medic in Vietnam. Although he would never talk about it, I'd hear family members talk saying that he didn't sleep well at night.

With all of my step-mom's siblings and cousins coming over, even though she didn't drink or smoke or curse, there was a party going on every weekend. They would gather and dance and play cards, etc. But I only experienced a part of that on a limited basis, based on whether or not we knew where they lived at the time. And then we would spend weekends together. And that would go on for a few months and then either they would move or we would move and then we'd lose touch again for five or six years.

How did I feel about that? That was just a way of life. As a kid I just went with it. It was not uncommon that I went to school and came home from school to find out, "Oh, we don't live there anymore."

In hindsight, I believe God allowed it to bring me to that place of strength that I'm in now because we live in a world that changes constantly. It never stops. Change . . . it's continual. And I think the Lord allowed that when I was growing up so that I wouldn't be a person who can't adapt.

My father ended up passing in August of 1998. And my grandmother had passed in April of 1998. And my mom died in '82. He was at my mother's funeral and he was at my grandmother's funeral. He still spoke very highly of both my grandparents. He never had an unkind word to say about either of them, and vice versa.

o   Two Incomplete Models – Mike

I never really knew my biological father because my parents separated when I was two years old. I had occasional phone contact with him until I was about 12. Then I didn't meet him until I was a junior in college, and I happened to go out to a fraternity conclave at San Antonio, Texas, as a delegate and he was a resident of El Paso. So, I extended my stay and drove down and stayed with him and his second wife. I met my two half-brothers. It turned out to be a really bad experience.

My mom had always spoken very highly of him, even though she was married to my step-father, Patrick. So I had this idealized view of him – a man who was very neat, never needed to have a watch for his time, etc. So I think my mom had a greater natural affection for him than she did for my stepfather; I could feel that as a son. So while she had been telling me all that, she inadvertently gave me the message that she didn't have a lot of respect for my stepfather—who was an alcoholic, uneducated, and uncouth in a lot of ways. He'd had difficulty coming back from the war in Vietnam where he served in very violent situations—killed a lot of people. He used to tell me about that when I was very young and he was drunk. That really shaped who I became later.

But when I was 20 and meeting my biological father, everything that I'd worked so hard for to bring honor to my mom, and even to my stepfather, I took in a binder to show my biological father and he didn't want to see it. He wanted to say bad things about my mom and we almost got into a fist fight; it really got kinda' ugly.

From that point on, I really didn't want to have that much contact with him. I tried, but he was so negative, and he was such a womanizer. I mean even when I was there he was kinda' eyeing other women, asking me, "What d'you think?" And then when we got in the argument in front of his house, he accused my mom of having cheated on him. But even 20 years later you could really peg it—he just had a wandering kind of eye. And my mom is this straight laced Asian woman. And so I figured, it was better that I didn't grow up under this man.

But as for my non-biological father, Patrick, I think my mom married him, initially, because she knew that I needed a father and he was a kind man. So when she came to the States and we went to Monterey Seaside she ended up meeting him in the mess hall—she worked in the mess halls (military cafeterias). I remember when they first dated, when I was three years old; they married when I was around five. It was good for me to have a father around.

He was a Drill Sergeant. I remember often times waking up at 5 in the morning to take his Smoky-the-Bear hat out of the press and give it to him. He dressed up in his fatigues, and he'd go to Fort Ord to train the new recruits and stuff. Those were positive things for me. It blended in with the negatives – the times he got drunk and embarrassed the family and stuff like that. But it probably wasn't good for me that my mother didn't have the level of respect for him that she should have. Outwardly she did, but I could just sense that it wasn't there.

Of course, they weren't believers at that time. And they were trying to do the best they could. My mom only made it to the third grade; my dad to the sixth. So once I made it to about the sixth grade, my parents couldn't help me with school any more. And so I often found father-figures outside the family and in men who were the school counselor or the dean or a girlfriend's father—constantly looking for other men to fill in for me and teach me life and what to do. It's an empty quest in a lot of ways.

So it was confusing for me with a father who didn't know how to take care of my mother in ways that she wanted. A classic example was when I was in high school and my mom drove a Pontiac which had a lot of transmission problems. She had to drive quite a distance from Salinas to Monterey and she'd have different difficulties with the car. My dad could fix things, but he never fixed it for my mom. But then he sold the car to a family friend—this guy we called Big Mike. I was Little Mike. He sold it to him at a steal and then spent the next two or three days in the driveway fixing the very transmission problem that he should have fixed for my mom – getting himself tired and not being able to work in the store (we owned a convenience store in Monterey). So then I had my mom saying, "I don't know why you fixed it for him; you never fixed it for me." So dad cared for the needs of those outside the family, but not my mom. That still hampers me today, because I am very sensitive to other people and will try to fill those needs and try to help people when it's not my job. It gets me in trouble.

Then when my dad was telling me he that loved me and stuff, he was usually drunk as a skunk and telling me how good a mom I have and how "She deserves better than me. You're a good son." And then he told me stories of people he'd killed over in Vietnam; he really had a lot of problems from that.

When I got out of college and I was searching for different things to do I left Chubb Insurance and went to work for Dale Carnegie & Associates, mainly because my dad had taken a Dale Carnegie course, and it had helped him to stop drinking and to feel good about himself. I was inspired that it could do that for my dad so I wanted to become a Dale Carnegie instructor. You can see the power later on in my life of wanting to understand my dad better. So I became a Dale Carnegie instructor based on that.

INTERNALIZED IMPACTS

"You know that feeling where, no matter what you do or where you go, you don't fit in? Don't know the word for that. Alienation? Estrangement? Incompatibility? Naw. That ain't right. But there's gotta' be a word for it, 'cause that's how I feel all the time."

—Akeelah and the Bee

o   Father-Figure Lovers – Giji

I was 16 when I entered the fun and frightening world of dating. Having both a physiology and vocabulary that belied my age, combined with the absence of a father to guide and protect my emergence into womanhood, I was a prime target for attracting the attention of much older men. The first who persisted was a co-worker at my first job at Sears.

Even I thought he was too old, and remembered thinking the first time he hit on me: "You should be ashamed; you're old enough to be my father." As it turned out, the scar on his face aged him by 10 years, so he wasn't as old as I thought he was. So, despite his marital status, that first ride to work rapidly led to my first lunch date, which led to my first kiss in the freight elevator, which evolved nine months later into my first sexual encounter—with a man 14 years my senior. He was old enough that, for the first several months after we were dating, I still could only call him Mr. Smith.

You may be reading this and wondering, what on earth would attract me to a man that age? Well, he'd had intriguing life experiences that he was willing to share with me. He possessed practical wisdom in areas of interest to me—he taught me a lot about bartending. He was incredibly chivalrous. Even though our relationship was on the down-low as far as my mother was concerned, he was publicly demonstrative in his show of preference and adoration for me with his siblings, in-laws, and colleagues. He provided financial support, even, and took care of all my car repairs. After being separated for just a few months when I went to college, he drove from South Florida early one Friday morning to surprise me and take me out to dinner in D.C. We spent the next three days in Virginia, completely consumed with each other. Our relationship lasted, in some iteration, from my junior year in high school through my sophomore year in college. He died unexpectedly in a car accident the following summer.

Since he was married, ours was obviously not an "exclusive" relationship. Besides, I could not take him to prom or grad night, so I did date a couple of guys in high school and my freshman year in college who were my age. But, throughout college, I found that most of the men I dated were seven to nine years my senior. I also noticed that after meeting my father, many of them started looking more and more like him, whereas the earlier ones tended to look more like my brother.

One admonition my mother shared with me, after I completed the Dwayne and Jean-Robert dating cycles in 12th grade—short-lived relationships with two popular 22-year-olds—was, "Your father would never have let you go out with half these guys you've picked." I've never forgotten that. I, too, had longed for my father to help me make better decisions about boyfriend selections—especially in the case of Dwayne, who tried to rape me the first and last time we officially "went out." A fact I've never shared with anyone. And his was not the only encounter of the "almost-violated-kind," from which I had no father to rescue me, and which I suffered in silence.

o In the Absence of Guidance– Kellee

When I think back on things, I really wish that he had been around. I probably wouldn't have run the streets as much as I did. I probably would have known what my worth was a whole lot earlier. I probably would have waited longer to have sex—I was 15, and maybe I would have waited until I was married. I just think there were a lot of things I would have waited for had he been around.

Even though my dad may have known more at the time, he wasn't really there to give me the spiritual guidance—except in the letters he wrote all throughout 10 years. He even sent me stuff about Jesus being my father. But it didn't sink in. I still ran the streets. I still had sex. I still dealt with homosexuality. I did all that. I did everything BUT get pregnant.

I know when I was a teenager how much I used to make fun of God and be the jokester saying things like, "Oh, you know you shouldn't be doing this; God's gonna' get you." And I would be in a circle with a bunch of people who were having a smoking fest; I'm not the one smokin', they are, but I'm the one making the jokes, and they'd say, "Oh, you better not do that, you better back away from her 'cause God's gonna' strike her dead right now." Probably would not have been so inclined to mock God, either, had my father been around.

o   Learning to Wait – Felecia

My father would say, "I'm coming to pick you up," and I'd have my bag ready and I'd wait. And he wouldn't come. I was 10, 11, 12 – and I'd wait. And he wouldn't come. That's the age when young ladies have to be close and spend time with the fathers. He wouldn't show up, wouldn't call, wouldn't send somebody. And my mom would be livid! She was very expressive and she'd say what I was feeling. I would internalize it. And because he was my father, I'd say, "He's coming." And when he didn't, I'd just shrug it off. But, it taught me to wait.

o   Fragile Family Ties – Kellee

My mom was always great. She wasn't like other mothers where the father goes away, they go to jail, and she has some animosity towards him and kept me away from him. She never did that. She dated. And I remember one time with a friend of hers, she said, "Get in the car; we're going on a little vacation." And they didn't want to tell me where we were going. And this was the first year that my father was locked up and he was way up state somewhere. And they surprised me that I was going to see my dad. That was really fun.

Then he was moved from up state down to Staten Island, which was a little bit closer to get to. It was still like three trains and two buses, but it was closer than going all the way up state. So, she took me to visit him at least twice a year. I remember one time, my brother and I were actually able to go there together.

My brother's mother encouraged the separation between him and our dad. She did not give all of my father's letters to my brother and she just let him feel angry. My brother was really angry that my dad wasn't around and she didn't help nurture him out of that. Even to this day, he doesn't really want to be associated with our dad. He'll say, "Oh yeah, I'm going to call you." Or he'll mention that he, my father, and I need to get together and have a sit-down and talk – this is what my brother tells me. Yet, he ran into our dad not too long ago on the streets of New York, gave our dad his number, our dad called him a couple of times, and my brother's not returning his phone calls. And when I speak to my brother, it's always, "I've been busy." He'll always do these things where he initiates it, but he doesn't really mean it. Or he doesn't ever have the time, so he says.

I was sad when my father was put away. Of course, I missed him, but I think I was more sad *for* him. I felt really awful that he was in that place. Because my father's a loving person, and I've heard horror stories about jails, I was always afraid of his being mistreated. He would tell me sometimes that his cell mates would see my picture and make derogatory comments and that made him feel uncomfortable, and it made me feel uncomfortable, too. But I mostly felt really bad for him.

o   Manhood Markers– Alex

With me, I guess, growing up without a father, I kind of started to question certain things—my validity as a son, as a young man—I started to wonder if there's something wrong with me. I grew up with a complex, like I felt disadvantaged.

So I guess it kinda' hampered a certain aspect of my development and my personality. For instance, when you play sports you engage in teamwork, building leadership qualities, just bringing out your personality interacting with different people. I grew up kinda' anti-social, so I wouldn't open up to a lot of people. I was very shy with very low confidence. Looking back now, I would say that was probably the result of not having a father figure or a man in my life to kind of affirm my identity and affirm who I am and show me what it means to be a man—that kind of stuff.

o   Men in Authority – Isaiah

The traumatic events that I remember from my childhood really shaped my relationship with men in authority. By the time I got to age 14, I was a raging inferno. I would rebel against my male teachers – I would just go at 'em. And I didn't realize it was because I was angry with my father, but I couldn't dare express that to him, 'cause you'd get knocked into next week. Then, they didn't have "time-outs," they had "knock-outs." You couldn't just express that. But I was very angry. And it carried through high school. It carried through college and in my first several jobs. I had a very difficult time working with any male authority. That anger really didn't get addressed until he had quadruple by-pass surgery in 1999. So you could say I went from 1970 to 1999 having a very distant, cold, and aloof relationship with my father.

I had a difficult time with our pastor because he was a man in authority. All the little things would come up. It was hard to trust the Lord that He would actually give me anything that I actually wanted, because my father thinks, some kind of way, if people want something, don't give it to them because it builds character.

o   The Making of a Man – Mike

My own stepfather, Patrick, didn't know the scriptures, and he didn't know our Heavenly Father, so he was vacant there, too. I now understand that. But as a result, as a teenager, I was creating a path from my own mind of what I should be doing to become a man.

I'd say the main way I tried to explore my development as a man was through my performance in high school—I always took leadership positions. I went to an all-male Catholic high school. I was the student body vice president and president. I was a varsity wrestler; I was on the varsity football team.

I often felt pressure to take care for others as part of growing into manhood. I didn't feel okay, unless I was doing things. I performed top in all my classes. At the same time I would hold study groups to help other perform well – I was like the go-to-guy to learn the study materials. I got a lot of kudos for that from school administrators and my girlfriend's father at that time. Unfortunately, people took advantage of that; I didn't know how to say, "no." I still have to deal with that.

I completely bought into the view that there was redemption through sexuality; I actually thought I was doing women a favor. That was clearly a part of being a man—if I could please a woman. That was further reinforced at Stanford by sociological professors.

Being tough and fearless also, I felt, were critical to being a man. I did a lot of martial arts—judo, wrestling, aikido. I was never fearful of other people. I knew my ability to harm them and how they could harm me. That was actually some of the reason I thought I could handle being a police officer.

My dad used to fight a lot as a kid. I didn't – I could talk people out of fighting me. I had a verbal skill my father didn't. One piece of advice my father gave me I've never forgotten is: "If you're ever in a fight, never show mercy to your opponent in a fight. You want him to give up the will to win." I know it sounds a bit warped, but there's a brutality in that, which gave me the confidence to feel comfortable among other men. That ability also allows me not to hurt the person who is not really a threat.

I did a lot of drinking with the guys—especially at one of the stud football player's house. Kind of a high school thing. I could get beer from our own store. My parents were kinda' hands-off. I wouldn't drink and drive; and I wouldn't let other people, but we'd go to parties all over.

I remember one time we went to Lake Naciemento when I was 16 or 17 years old. I was drinking **with** my dad and my girlfriend. And then he let me sleep in the same tent with my girlfriend. He exposed me to the underside of life with these people—I think that's part of why my mom didn't respect my dad.

I do have sweet memories of riding motorcycles with my dad and camping. My dad and I used to go to Fort Hunter Liggit and shoot hundreds, if not thousands, of ground squirrels. That was definitely a part of being a man. I developed my marksmanship skill. So that was kind of a guy thing.

I would read a lot of self-help books, like Leo Buscaglia; I was trying to get help understanding how to be a person—how to interact with people.

But as I grew up, I really had a lot of contempt for my dad because he didn't seem to meet my mom's needs a lot. So I became "parentifide" very early on; I performed well to please my mom, so that she would have a satisfaction in life that really she should have gotten from our Heavenly Father and from her own husband.

I still try not to fall under that trap. And I don't know why I try to excel sometimes. Is it because I hear the voice of God to do something or because I feel like I have to fulfill the expectations or to meet the needs of someone who's hurting, like my mom, when it really isn't my job to fulfill?

I notice it with my own kids now when, sometimes if Selina's upset or something, or if I'm upset, my kids will try to change the environment to make me happy or to make my wife happy. And I try as gently as possible to say, "Aw, don't worry. You're kids, and this really isn't on you. I have my own issues, and right now I'm not very happy, but it's not because of you. And I'll make it through this; you just enjoy being a kid." My parents didn't have the wherewithal to do that.

o   Doorway to the Occult – Giji

I spent every summer with my great-grandmother—Motherdear—for the first nine-and-a-half years of my life. She was the center of my world during that time and had the most impact on my spiritual development then. What I took note of most was that "church" and "religion" were not just Sunday rituals for Motherdear, but church came to her house. I would regularly help her make pies to host the Women's Circle meetings at her house and, if it were not past my bedtime, sometimes she would allow me to listen in from the dining room table on the exhortation they shared with each other from the Bible.

After Motherdear died, there was a void of God-consciousness in my world for several years. I remember that my grandfather read the Bible at home every day, but I only saw him during summers and holidays and he didn't really talk about the Word with me. Even though my mother had married a pastor, there was no evidence that I could see, of a daily involvement with God in her life.

I recall being unable to sleep one night at my grandmother's house around the age of 11 and she told me to repeat Psalm 23 until I fell asleep. When I told her I didn't know it, she disapprovingly responded, "What? Your mother hasn't taught you Psalm 23? What is she doing?" That let me know that my mother had definitely been taught the Bible at some point, and that there was some expectation by her parents of her passing that legacy to her children. Somewhere I remember hearing that my mother and her siblings had attended Vacation Bible School. I was never introduced to those kinds of activities.

When I was in high school, I remember expressing surprise at the fact that my mother had ordered a return address label for herself with a Christian symbol on it. She was really upset with me when I honestly shared my marvel, but I felt like, "How could I – would I have expected that?" I'd never seen or heard her do anything outside of a church to identify herself as a Christian.

What was common, with the mixture of Native American spiritual stuff floating in my family, was the acknowledgment of spiritual visitations by deceased relatives, and the like. Everyone seemed to accept it pretty readily, except Auntie Marian, who had left the family church and adopted Roman Catholicism as the conduit for her faith. I remember very clearly someone saying that Uncle Bubba had come to see them the night before and sat on their bed. All I could think was, "I'm glad he didn't come to see me." But this was one siting of many over the years. I honestly thought this was a very normal part of everyone's family life, until I got to college.

During my last year of high school, I had several encounters with cats through which I would get this sort of "prophetic message" from my deceased great-grandmother. I really can't explain it. But no one in my family flinched or questioned it when I shared these revelations—all of which did contain accurate pieces of information I could not have known.

I had been an avaricious reader and generally curious about all spiritual things from a very young age. Some elements the Lord shielded me from altogether, *e.g.* the actual church of Satan. I went to a B. Dalton bookstore, somewhere between age 11 and 13, and found myself checking out the spiritual section, which was not uncommon. To my amazement, they actually had a copy of *The Satanic Bible* on the shelf. Even though I'd heard of it, I really didn't expect to find it available on sale at your local neighborhood bookstore. So, out of curiosity, I picked it up.

When I opened what looked like the front of the book, the text appeared to be written upside down. Before I could adjust it, the book, literally, **leapt** of my hand. I looked around to see if the other people perusing books in that section had noticed what had just happened. I turned, walked very quickly out of the bookstore, and never had the desire pick up that book again. In fact, it was years before I would reenter another B. Dalton bookstore. My mother commented that this was first time she'd ever seen me leave a bookstore and she didn't have to hunt me down among the shelves to leave the mall. I never talked with her about it, but I was scared straight.

So after my brief experience with getting to know Jesus at the age of 13, the person who had the most influence on my life, overall, was my brother Dana, eight years older than me. I idolized him—I think literally and figuratively. He was a fount of wisdom and compassion, and I was fully confident of his unconditional love for me. As he went through various spiritual explorations, I followed.

First, following his example, I took a seven-month path to becoming a vegetarian—not because of my own convictions, but because of his. Then, just before I went to college, he introduced me to Hindu chanting. I found myself seeking out ashrams in New York and Maryland to join chant sessions and partake of organic vegetarian food.

Definitely not the likely path of a "pk" had the "p" been around.

TURNING POINTS

Hallie/Annie: ". . . And if you ask me, a dad is an irreplaceable person in a girl's life . . . . Just imagine someone's life without a father. Never buying a father's day card. Never sitting on their father's lap. Never being able to say, 'Hi Dad. What's up Dad? Or catch you later, Dad.' . . . ."

Nick Parker: "Let me see if I get this: You missed being able to call me, 'Dad'?"

Hallie/Annie: "Yeah, I really have, Dad."

—The Parent Trap

o The Phone Call – Giji

Graduation was an unusually hectic time for my family because my brother, Dana, was graduating from college in north Florida, the same weekend I was graduating from high school in south Florida, and my school's Award's Night preceded his graduation. That meant that my grandparents, aunts, uncles, cousin, and niece who were celebrating with us traveled from the West Coast of Florida down to Ft. Lauderdale one day, we all went up to Tallahassee the next, and all came back to Ft. Lauderdale the day after that. By the time we were back in Ft. Lauderdale for my graduation, I had not heard anything from my father. I don't remember feeling one way or another about it at the time – maybe because there was so much activity surrounding these occasions. But I imagine that, at the same time, I was suppressing fear of rejection; I was determined to believe that my father wanted to see me as much as

I wanted to see him and he just hadn't received the invitation yet. After all, I hadn't done anything to cause the separation.

We had an apartment full of people with all of the relatives in town, and the telephone had been ringing off the hook, with many of the calls having been for me – the graduate. But when it rang early that evening before graduation day, I suspected that it was probably for Mommie – all of my friends were doing things with their families that night, she talked on the phone as much if not more than I did, and I figured, by then, I had talked to all of my relatives who were not in town.

"Hello," I answered – fully prepared to call for Mom to let her know who was on the phone for her.

"Hello. May I please speak to Kha or Giji?" this unfamiliar man's voice said. (And while he seemed a stranger, I suddenly had butterflies in my stomach.)

"This is Giji," I said with pleasant curiosity.

Pause. "Hi. This is Mr. Deadwyler."

After gulping some air, and with increasing anxiety, I responded, "Which Mr. Deadwyler?" Even though I knew it wasn't Daddy Ed's voice, my brain couldn't reconcile the possibility that it might be . . .

"This is Bobby. This is your father."

Anyone inside my mind would have thought for sure he or she was in an echo chamber. "This is your father" bounced back and forth between my ears finding no place of rest. I don't know how long it was before I heard through the handset still plastered to my ear, "Giji, are you there? Are you alright?" It was only then that I realized I was standing paralyzed with tears streaming down my face. I wanted to shout, "Daddy!?!" but I couldn't open my mouth; it was frozen in awe.

Not wanting him to hang up due to my sudden verbal impotence and lose the only connection I'd ever known with my father, I hurried (as best I could under the circumstances) to find my mother. As I look back now, I can only see it in slow motion. Since I still couldn't speak, I tapped her on her shoulder to get her attention. I think she was in the middle of a conversation, but I can't be sure because "This is your father" was still ringing in my ears above the din in the living and dining rooms. I knew I probably looked crazy and didn't want her to be alarmed or frightened by my silent tears, but I couldn't do anything about them at the time. When she suddenly realized I was crying, she asked, "Giji, what's wrong? What is it?" – at which point I shoved the sweaty receiver in her hand.

I walked with her and remember her saying, "Hello!? Oh, Hi! Yes, she'll be okay. I think she's probably just a bit overwhelmed." At that point, I really lost it. I slipped out from my mother's arm around my waist and ran to my room to find solace in sobbing into my pillow, I guess, until I fell asleep. I have no recollection of any conversation about that night with anyone for many years.

o They Say the Third Time's a Charm – Alex

I guess the second or the third time I went I was about 16 or so. And my uncle went with me 'cause we were checking on some schools, or something like that. We stayed at his place. And I would say that was the beginning of reconnecting with him, probably because my uncle—my mom's brother– was there. My dad's family's all in Guyana. I guess my uncle had a better idea of why he left in the first place.

I can remember my dad and I were in a restaurant, and we were talking, and I think I brought up the issue. I think I asked him, "So why did you leave? Or why did you abandon us?"

Then he was like, "Oh I never abandoned you. Certain things just didn't work out."

And I guess I was really angry at that point, and my uncle was there. So he sat me down in the restaurant and said, "Listen, he didn't abandon you. Things didn't work out." Hearing that from my uncle I kinda' believed it a little bit more. At some point I have to learn to forgive. I think that was the point where I kinda' let go of that resentment, and I started to get to know him a little better.

o The Wedding – Fran

In July of 1991, I had an aunt who had gotten married, and I was in the wedding, so we went over to my aunt's house the day after the wedding. The family was just gathering over there still in celebration. It just so happened that my mother and my father had started talking again, in the dating sense – which was weird – so he happened to be over there with her. My dad and I ended up together in the kitchen alone, and we just started talking.

Of course he had been drinking. My father started smoking and drinking when he was 13 years old, so he'd always been a drinker. From the time he would get up in the morning, not too long after, he would pretty much start drinking.

Anyway, I knew he had been drinking some and by that time I was saved and God had started doing a lot of healing in my heart, especially about the past with my father – with my mother, too, there was a whole lot that went on with that. But we started talking and he really started expressing how he always felt like I hated him. He shared all these emotions about how he felt about me and how he thought I felt about him.

So my response was, "I was a stupid little kid; I probably did hate you. But I don't hate you now. I love you."

It really broke something in him. It did something in the relationship where I don't know that he ever heard me tell him I love him, because I don't think I ever did tell him I loved him. That was the kind of the whole thing surrounding the "reunion" of sorts.

After that, he felt more comfortable calling me; he felt more comfortable coming to see me. I remember I moved to a different apartment, and he actually came to see me at my apartment. I mean I'm a grown woman, and I couldn't actually remember a time when he had come see me when I was living alone. I even remember when I moved over there. I had this old clunker car and it was parked for a long time in one space and, you know, people pay attention to that. Someone stole the battery out of my car. And during this time when my father was talking to me and coming to see me I was just telling him, in passing, that somebody stole my battery. Much to my surprise—he didn't even tell me he was going to—he bought a new battery, brought it over, and put the battery in my car. So there were times he would respond to things . . . I really didn't ask him directly, but . . . he would just do stuff. He would initiate contact, come over and visit. And I started to go over to visit the family more.

o   Out of the Ashes – Isaiah

In 1997, I was a Christian and volunteering full-time for a missionary organization. I was going through some of my belongings and I found a picture of my father. By the way, I hadn't spoken to him on a regular basis since about 1978, so it'd been about 19 years. It was a portrait of him—one of those head shots you take in a suit for your career. And I felt the Holy Spirit say, "You've got to get things straight with this man." I said, "Okay, Lord, if You want to get my relationship straight, I'm going to ask You to do whatever You have to do." And I wasn't really moving real fast in that direction.

Then in 1999, my father had a quadruple by-pass. He had what they call "the widow-maker." If he had had a full-blown heart attack, he would have been dead before he hit the ground. I think the **least** blocked artery was maybe at 85 percent. The doctor said when he opened up my dad's aorta, cholesterol looked like chunks of cheese passing through his heart.

My brother was raising his family, and he lived too far away. And my sister lived up north. So it was left to me to help take care of my dad after the open-heart surgery.

The first day that I had to go over there, he called me up at 6 o'clock in the morning cussing me out. "Get your a## over to my house!" And get me my f@!★#%^ breakfast! You better go to IHOP." He was screamin' and hollerin' over the phone.

I was thinking, "This man's crazy!" This is when I'm in my forties. And I said to myself, "Fool, don't you know I could put ground glass in your food. You just had open-heart surgery; nobody's going to question it if you die. What kind of fool are you?"

So I got there. Once I got in, after he hollered "Is my food right?", he went on a 20 minute tirade. "I don't like you. I think you're arrogant." And all these things he didn't like.

To both our amazement, I replied, "Well listen – I don't like you either. And you're not going to intimidate me today." I said, "You're selfish, you're stingy—you have a heart like a lump of coal. And if you don't like it, tough; I'm not going anywhere." And we glared at each other for about three hours, until it was time for my Mom to take over.

It went like that for about two weeks. So I went in one day and I was loaded for bear, as usual. My dad was sitting up in his bed and he was grinning from ear-to-ear. I said, "What are you smiling about?"

He said, "God did this!"

I said, "God? God did what?"

"God let me have that open heart surgery so our relationship could be restored."

And I was thinking, "I can't believe my father said that." I was in shock.

He went on to say, "Yeah, I always wanted to be close to you, and all of a sudden all that stuff from when I was a kid started hitting me in my forties." He wondered why we didn't talk very much. How come

I didn't ask his advice about stuff. For the first time, my dad expressed how much he wanted to be involved in my life.

I didn't think he cared, but actually those 20 years of silence were getting to him. And I didn't tell him, "Well, you were such a jerk I didn't want to be bothered with you." But actually he started turning a little bit; he got a little bit better.

But then my mother's illness got worse and he got more controlling. My mother died in 2009. Riding home from the funeral, my dad said, "You know Isaiah, everybody that ran into your mother said that they became closer to God because of their contact with her. She was my wife for 53 years, and I want to get closer to God, too." He described how my mother, wracked with pain curled in a fetal position, cried out, "I love Jesus! I love Jesus!" He said, "I can't say that I love Jesus, but I want to. I want to go to heaven to prove to your mom how much I loved her." My dad had done a 180.

In fact, he said, "You know, Isaiah. I've been a jerk." He said, "I know I've done stuff to hurt people." He said, "I'm trying to change." He said, "Losing your mom, I realize that relationships aren't permanent, and that the people that you love you need to keep close to you and let them know that you love them."

I can honestly say that my father has been trying to change. He's changed in a lot of ways; he actually called me up to see how I was doing—that had never happened. But my mother's death really opened up his eyes and he realized he had some good kids. And even though I didn't do what he felt was best with my life, I'm doing what I feel is best and that's okay.

As we talked more, one of his frustrations was he said, "Isaiah, you're my best and my brightest; you could have done anything you wanted to do."

I said, "Well, Dad, I'd planned to go to law school. I didn't plan to be a missionary. I had planned to retire by the age of 50. As a majority stock-holder in my law firm, I was supposed to have a home in Hawaii and a home in the Bahamas. Basically, I'd planned to be on my sailboat – you weren't going to see me. It wasn't my game plan to be a missionary." But I said, "God placed me here. And because He's placed me here, I'm faithful to Him." I said, "There's a lot of dying you do following Jesus with your whole heart. You die to your own personal dreams, but God gives you a better reality." With that, I think he began to understand a little bit about my life, although he doesn't understand a lot about it. But I think, in his own way, he kinda' respects it.

After that, I enjoyed the time that I spent with him. It wasn't frequent, but when I did, I was not looking for him to approve of me. I realized it was not about me, really, it was about him and how I could help him. That's helped heal my wounds. But it was really the Holy Spirit who changed my heart—because I was very angry and I was very bitter. If the Holy Spirit hadn't done what He was doing, my relationship would never have gotten restored.

o First, the Name Change ~ Mike

After about the first three years of my coming to faith in Christ, I read through my Bible and came to understand the concept of being adopted into the family of God. I felt conviction from the fifth command to honor my father and mother. As a result, I decided to go through an adult adoption in 1998. Patrick was honored that I would just think about it. And I remember I notified my biological father. I was making a very clear statement to Patrick. "I'm going to bear your name – this is part of me honoring you." I had to have all my uniforms and name tags changed. Now, legally, he's my dad. Abe was three years old by then—we only recently changed his and Ruthie's name last name to O'Coffey.

o The Preparations ~ Giji

Now that I think about it, I don't remember talking with my father on the phone again. At some point–who knows–maybe that same night, my mother communicated to me that he could not come to the graduation although he would have loved to. He actually had just left Miami, Florida the day he called to return to Atlanta, only to find the graduation invitation awaiting. He had no idea where we were. With that piece of news, I couldn't help but feel this gripping sense of being unjustly robbed rising up within me. But after seventeen years of no communication, there was no point in being disappointed about this particular unfortunate set of circumstances over which I had had no control. In any event, he would be coming to see me, if that was all right with Mommie and me, of course, in July.

My mind draws a complete blank concerning anything that took place in my life between graduation day and the days we began making preparations for his visit. I couldn't really read what my mother was feeling about the whole matter, although I sensed she was trying to be supportive. She even bought me Rod McKuen's book, *Finding My Father*. This I found somewhat odd because until now, she had not expressed any hope that one day my father and I might have a relationship. But neither of us asked what the other was thinking and feeling (as I recall), nor offered of herself the same.

Those last couple of days before his arrival playback only in slow motion. There are no sounds or smells associated with that time. I don't remember the specifics of any conversation I had with my mom about anything, although we must have talked details because I remember that we came to some agreement about what we would have for dinner the day he arrived–of course, I can't remember what we cooked. Mostly, I remember cleaning. Cleaning like I had never done before. I especially remember the dreaded white naugahyde couch, which had been my least favorite item in the house to clean, because that day I really didn't mind. I cleaned and cooked myself to the point of exhaustion.

Pivotal Pillars

"I wouldn't underestimate the power of fathers. They're good for picking you up and dusting you off. They give you the courage to do things you thought you never could."

— The Game Plan

Often, because he didn't treat us the way we felt a father should treat us, we developed bitterness, hatred, and unforgiveness toward or disregard for him. Facing this pain as an adult means that, in some way, we've been off-kilter all these years. Many times we tried to substitute and find somebody who would replace him to make us feel whole. And they didn't do it either because they're just human, too.[1] One survey indicated that only **34%** of adult males could say that they considered their own father to be a role model.[2]

Your relationship with and your feelings toward your father are like the load-bearing walls that are essential in building a safe and secure house. If you've worked diligently at reconciling your relationship with your father, then you have a firm foundation from which to begin parenting your own children. Although walls, in the context of parenting, often conjure the negative connotation of boxing your children in with rigid absolutes and the prohibition of free thinking, those same walls help protect and define. "A father who practices the principles of effective fathering will help a child always know where 'home' is, no matter how far that child might wander."[3]

o A Suitable Surrogate – Giji

Even when I went to college and my newfound relationship with my father was hundreds of miles away, God filled the father hole with another—Professor Samuel F. Yette. He was the quintessential male nurturer – mostly of learning. But I'll never forget the day I was low in spirit and delayed my departure from his class. He was very in tune with his students and recognized my unusual lack of participation in class as a sign of something being wrong in my world. As he approached my seat, he gently inquired, "Are you okay Miss Dennard? Are you sick? Having boy troubles?" While I wasn't quite prepared to open up at that moment (I did eventually), it was incredibly reassuring to know that I had a father figure nearby to whom I could turn for comfort and counsel.

o The Father Fill-In – Alex

I really respect my uncle. My uncle's been like my father figure for most of my life. My family all lived together. He was the only male. He set the example. He's very successful, works with gas companies, is the head of accounting, the head of a Rotary Club. So I kinda' look up to him both as an educational example because he's a very intelligent guy, the way he interacts with people, how he handles leadership. He's a Christian – so that was a really good example for me. Whenever you needed him, he was there. He would actually pick up the slack, like if I needed extra classes. The way it works in Trinidad, he worked on one end and my school was all the way at the other end, so it took at least three hours to get to my school. So he would leave work, pick us up, take us to lessons, get us "sump'in ta eat," and hang out—which he didn't have to do at all. He's just an uncle. Rarely do you find uncles taking up that kinda' slack. Even with bills and stuff, he would help my mom out.

o My Papa – Felecia

As far as having a sense of who I am, in terms of that daughter-father relationship, and the other things that helped shape my identity came from my grandfather, because he was absolutely the most beautiful man that ever lived. And I'm sure there are a lot of people who can say that about different male role models in their lives. But my grandfather—he was my father, he was my friend, he was my grandfather, he was my confidant, he was just the ultimate of what you could ask for in a dad. My mom would get in a jam and couldn't pay her rent, my grandfather would step up and pay her rent for months and months ahead, buy food, and make sure that we had lights, and that kind of thing.

Now there came a point in time when he stepped back and forced my mother to grow up. And we felt it when he did that. My grandfather— never ever once did I hear him say an unkind word about my father. He just stepped up. He never once said, "Well, this is what he should be doing" or "that's what he's supposed to do." He never did that.

My grandfather was an entrepreneur and he was a blessed man of God. And I truly believe that's where I get my entrepreneurial spirit from. Because there were times that I would spend hours and hours with him at his store. And I know that my first customer service experience was with him at five and six years old in his store down on U Street, which was the corridor for a lot of the black businesses back in the day.

VOICE OF THE FATHER

*"I don't want Jesi to suffer. I don't want her to make
the same mistakes her father did – of accepting life and
accepting situations. I want her to fight, and I want her
to win."*

– Bend It Like Beckham

Essentially, there are three kinds of fathers: there are natural fathers, there are spiritual fathers, and there is the Heavenly Father.

Fathers of this generation, and maybe a few past, have not lived up to their role as fathers, even though fathers are the key to our whole development. Furthermore, there are different shades of natural fathers. You've got progenitors, you've got adopters, you've got legal guardians, you've got surrogate, etc.[1]

Earthly fathers affect their "children's development in three main ways: spiritually, physically and emotionally."[2] That's why it is vital for the father to realize how significant his presence is in the home. Even before they get to be an independent church member, children look to their fathers for spiritual guidance. "Many children will follow in the footsteps of their fathers when it comes to a belief in God or not."[3]

"It is very common for children to think God values them in the same way their own fathers regard them." For instance, if Dad is loving, warm, and nurturing, the children tend to ascribe those same attributes to God. "But if Dad is perceived as cold, distant and occupied with 'more important things,' they are likely to feel that God is unapproachable and uninterested in them as individuals."[4]

All children tend to embrace the faith and mindsets of those by whom they feel the most loved. That's primarily because whoever has their heart has their ears. As a result, they are much more likely to accept the truth you impart if you deliver it to them within the context of a loving, heart-to-heart relationship. "Research shows that Christians are theologically losing the next generation. More than 90 percent of born-again kids today are rejecting the absolute truth their parents embrace."[5] Why? According to Josh McDowell, "You can be the greatest explainer of truth. But if the very heart of your son or daughter does not believe 'my Daddy loves me,' they will walk away from your truth."[6]

The second way the father affects his children is physically. "Yes, he helped create them when his sperm combined with the mother's egg and the baby was formed in the mother's womb, but the effect the father has on his children goes far beyond that. It goes to the way they act and think."[7]

The last major way that the father affects his children is emotionally. Schaller says, "Some fathers deplete rather than give. A father who beats, molests, verbally degrades, disrupts the stability of the home by his alcohol, gambling, drugs, or moodiness is an anti-father. He sucks the life from the veins of his family; he functions as an emotional black hole. He steals the carefree laughter of childhood. Such a father produces a large amount of psychic orphanhood in his children forcing them to function as emotional orphans even though both parents are still alive."[8] Specifically for girls, when Daddy disappears from his daughter's life, for whatever reason, he relinquishes one of the most significant roles he should play in her life: "the development of her autonomy and independence."[9]

Being a dad isn't just about paying the bills.[10] "They teach their girls who they are, can be, and are becoming, how to get where they want to go and what treatment to demand along the way. They teach their sons how to feel, think and act towards a woman, how to be a man, and how to serve God,"[11] all of which helps to build the child's self-esteem.

Guiding and guarding the preoccupations of your children which sway their hearts and minds is a key to successful fathering. Stephen and Alex Kendrick urge that is critical to constantly keep your eye on these six influences because any of them "can steal your children's hearts away from you, pollute their minds, and lead them away from God": their friends, their education, their music, the movies and TV they watch, the internet sites they surf, and the video games they play. The father has the responsibility, not only to lead them toward good friends, good books, good music, etc., but also to teach the child to ask questions like: "Is this honoring to God? Will this help me do the right things? Will this fuel my passion for Christ or will it pour cold water on it?"[12]

Shepherds – pastors and priests– are your spiritual fathers. Because so many people have had bad relationships with their natural fathers, they often have bad relations with their shepherd, and they have bad relationships with God; one reflects on the other.

The Heavenly Father is the father of all who are born-again. If you've had a difficult or non-existent relationship with your earthly father, you may be looking at our Heavenly Father from the perspective of "Look what I had to go through! If He loved me, why'd He do this?" The answer is simple: His ways are higher than our ways and His thoughts are higher than our thoughts. [Isaiah 55:9] Besides, He needs you as a tool, and you can't be a tool unless you've gone through some hardship. Otherwise, all the people who had those problems wouldn't be able to be reached because they'd always be able to say "I went through stuff that you can't even understand." So, sometimes, God has to put you in positions where you get done in, on purpose, so that you can overcome, and, in turn, teach others how they, too, can overcome. But God **always** means it for good. [Gen. 50:20]

Often you don't know what your father went through that brought him to that place of neglect. There is a righteous authority that God gives dads because of their role as father, but even if they're believers that doesn't make them perfect as fathers. He might be your father, but he's just another man.[13] And even if he were the worse father on the planet, Jesus died for him, too, so he deserves your mercy and forgiveness.

Fathers frequently know what kind of fathers they *want* to be, but they don't know how to be that. Particularly if their father wasn't any of those things when they were growing up, they often fear "that [they] would become more like him than the father [they] wanted to be.[14]

o The Fallen Frame – Bobby Deadwyler

February 25, 1961 . . . Because of an unidentifiable aspect of incompatibility, after several months of marriage, the verbal glue of our vows melted, and the pictorial framing of all the beautiful things we had hoped for fell from its wall of grace. Grace wasn't damaged; the frame fell!

At that time, I was pastoring John Wesley Methodist Church in East Rutherford, New Jersey. I was troubled and spiritually uncomfortable. You see, I had a wife somewhere who was pregnant, brave but hardheaded, trying to weather life's stormy complications on her own. I was not aware she was planning to leave until I returned from Wilmington, Delaware, where I had gone to perform the wedding ceremony of my best friend. I learned later she had gone to Washington, D.C., but her residence was unknown.

At the same time, my Methodist persuasion was going through a doctrinal re-examination, and I found myself saying, "Yes," to another set of spiritual tenets – the Church of God in Christ. As I shared this "conversion" with the entire body of the church, I saw some sadness turning into joys of understanding and respect. Even though I surrendered my pulpit back to the bishop of the church, I was asked to continue to come back there and preach. I did, but moved to Hackensack, New Jersey, and continued attending Manhattan Bible College in New York City.

Kha was resolutely attached to my heart, so every time I saw a mother with her child, the memory of Kha and her little boy Dana, of whom I was very fond, enveloped my mind. Soon conviction began to clench my conscience as the scriptures became more illuminated at the hearing. I took particular note of Paul's statement to the Colossians in the third chapter and nineteenth verse – "Husbands, love your wives, and be not bitter against them," and the exhortation by David in Proverbs 18:22 that "Whoso findeth a wife findeth a good thing, and obtaineth favour of the Lord." My indebtedness to God is so great; I couldn't afford to lose my place in His bosom.

So I started calling around in an effort to locate Kha, to find out if we could try to make it work. I discovered she was then living in St. Petersburg, Florida, with her parents, and a very beautiful, precious daughter of six months. Immediately, I was in contact with Kha to let her know I was headed in her direction.

o   Raising a Daughter – Perry Fuller

Personally, I think the most challenging thing, especially in dealing with Jasmine, is not to be overbearing and try to dictate what's she's doing, what time's she's doing it, how she's going to do it—really allowing her to have freedom of expression in her life and choose her route freely. At the same time, being able to give a lot of input into what she's doing, whether I'm doing it verbally or indirectly. I guess the biggest challenge is what most parents face: once she's of age, is she really prepared to be independent the way I think she is? I mean independent of me and Margot, loving outside the home by herself—like going to college. I think she will, but has she developed to the point that she's going to make mature decisions in handling life itself? Sometimes I can't help but wonder whether I allowed her to experience different things or have been dictator in her life and really restricted her growth, which I tried not to do. You see kids do things that you know are not going to really benefit them, but sometimes you have to sit back and allow them to learn for themselves.

As a Christian, my greatest desire for Jasmine is that she becomes a godly woman, that she respects herself and that she excels at anything she does. I mean the excelling part and the ambition part is there but I want to make sure she makes it to Heaven—that's my main thing. The most significant decision that she will make is whether she will continue to serve Jesus the rest of her life – and not just serve Him, but that her life will be a testimony of Him also.

Going away from home – meeting the fellas—hopefully she'll make the right decisions. After many talks with her and allowing her that freedom of movement, when she does leave, she won't feel like she's a free bird out of a cage now and do some crazy stuff. With her being a female and my being a male, you see things happening. But you can't force your decisions or how she feels about things happening. You just offer the input and hopefully she gains from it. I'd hate for her to have to go through things I've seen other girls go through. I used to be an instigator of things they went through.

If I could have 10 kids like Jasmine I'd have them. Everyone has his or her downfalls or shortcomings but, as a whole, I really appreciate Jasmine. I hope she continues to excel at what she does. She's turning out to be a pretty dependable, intelligent young lady, with a pretty nice personality and a concern and care for people. I see her interacting with her friends. My hope was that she would be a person that's amicable and friendly and know how to communicate with people and present herself in a friendly way.

Sometimes Margot and I call her Shirley, from "The Color Purple," where it says, "Surely Shirley, you mean and surly." So when she starts acting crazy, Margot and I call her Shirley.

When I grew up, I didn't have a father. My father died when I was eight years old. I guess that father-son relationship never really quite developed with him. So the concept of or saying "Heavenly Father" or praying to the Father – it took a while for me. Because my whole idea of what a father is or how to relate to a father, I didn't have that growing up so…it took a while to develop. I know when people used to call Pastor "Pops" or stuff like that, or call Vonda "Moms," I couldn't identify with that. I've told Vonda jokingly that it's hard to conceive of her as my mom – "You're so totally different from my mom." I could say it moreso to Pastor because he's done some things for me to help me in the past that I felt like my father would have helped me with if he had been living. So I'm more apt to call the pastor "Pops" than Vonda "Moms." I already have a mom, so my conception of what a mom is has already been formed, but the father thing, I had to develop that.

I can't always relate to how the Lord as Father looks at me being His child. But there is something there sometimes. When my daughter does something I don't really agree with, I had to learn through the years not to voice my opinion so strongly, but to hold back and allow her to grow, and realize she's going to make mistakes and it's not always for me to correct her or say anything to try to make her see my viewpoint. That took a while. About five or six years ago one time I hollered at Jasmine and she said "shhhh, shhhh." Then I caught myself – why are you hollering at this girl? I realized at that point that in being vocal with her I didn't want to wound her, so I stopped doing it. I realized that I was hurting her doing that and I haven't done it since. So even if she does something that I don't appreciate, I've come to the point that I'll try and explain it to her about what she did and why she did and not be to the point that I'm dramatic and mad. And rather than show my emotions and anger, try to be more from a teaching point of view. When she does something, I try to tell her why and how what she just did would appear to someone else and how it wouldn't work out positively for her in terms of what she wants to do. So I have to go from that angle – teacher / student. I think we've developed a better relationship by doing that.

By my doing that with her, I can see how the Lord puts up with a lot of mess from me that I've done in the past and not just jacked me or even just allowed me to go to hell. I see how He corrects me and still is loving at the same time.

I realize that being a father really affects a daughter's perspective in a dramatic way. I had to realize that I was going to be a big impact on this girl's life so I'd better get my act together. By "my act together" I mean my communication with her and how I interact with her – that I would make a positive impact on her life that she won't feel so needy that she would need that male companionship from somebody other than me.

Jasmine's hard to me, sometimes. I tell her sometimes that I feel like I have more communication with her buddies than I do with her. She's a kind of a private person. I can't get offended by that. If she allows me to open and talk, I will and she accepts it. But I'm not trying to push her to make her; I realize that may come in time. That may be another stage in her life. What I've seen over the last year or two is where she's really been trying to develop more of an interpersonal personal relationship talking with me – me moreso than Margot; she's always had it with her mother. I really pushed Margot to have the relationship with her because I wanted Margot to have a great impact on her development and who she is, so she would not seek her identity from TV, magazines, and stuff like that. Sometimes I feel like just throwing her out the window. I guess the Lord does the same thing with me. Some of the decisions, some of the things I end up doing, He's thinking, "That big-headed boy."

She's got her own agenda. She's acquired different friendships. I like her friends, for the most part. I try not to interfere. I'm more a background type person now. We don't really do a lot of things together. I feel like that's going to change in the short time we still have together. We don't go out and hang out and stuff like that. She's just becoming of an age where I feel like we can develop a friendship. Before, like I told her, I didn't really want to be your friend; I'm just trying to make sure you're doing the right thing. So I was always the one who had to correct her. I was always the one that had to say, "No." Margot made sure I was the one she had to come to and ask questions – the bad ones that she didn't want to say no to – I had to end up being the "punisher." For a couple years there I was saying, "Margot, this thing is getting uneven." I felt like she was looking to me as being the corrections officer and Margot being her buddy. I still think Margot does that to a point. When she doesn't want to say, "No," to her she says, "Ask your daddy." She knows I'm going to say, "No."

I've surprised her a few times and said, "Yes." I'd rather her experience things being at home while I'm watching it than being outside drowning and not being able to help her.

There's not so much I can say on certain things, but I'll go to her older cousins and say, "You need to talk to your cousin and school the girl; y'all need to talk to her. If she's falling by the wayside, I'm not taking that hit because you all have had different experiences that you should pass onto your younger cousin." I think she'll respect them more than if it's coming from me.

From talking to different sisters, I found out that the father's really the central part and figure in a daughter's life that God has and that there's a different kind of communication she'd have with the mom. I would be the one that stabilized her life – for the better or for the worse. And her interaction with other men would be based moreso from her relationship with me. So I wanted to make sure we had a good relationship and an open relationship. Not too open – but, an open relationship that she could build on so that when she did meet another guy she'd pull from those things that I've offered her or she's seen in me that she wants out of another man. That's why I had to change my approach with her, because I was being domineering. Being a restrictive type person, I had to start disengaging more of that part of my personality and being more of a friend and support role.

One day a few years back, we changed our minds about going to D.C. and she said, "I want to go shopping."

I said, "I don't want to go to no store."

She said, "Come on, walk with me; you never go shopping with me." She set me up. She said, "What do you think of this?" She tried it on. "Cause you're always complaining about my black jacket." She's got this old ugly black jacket. I said I was going to take it out of her closet and throw it away. So she said, "This could replace that jacket you don't like."

I said, "Yeah."

She said, "Buy it, then."

I reminded her that her grandmother had sent her some money.

She said, "Aw, that money's for something else."

So I ended up buying her the coat. Normally I would never have done it; it wasn't on sale any more. Margot and I trained her "if it's not on sale, don't even look at it." Sometimes you gotta' go against what you believe in order to reinforce the relationship. In my natural instincts I wouldn't have done it, but I had to think back and say "what kind of positive statement are you going to make by doing this for her?" You can't say because you don't have the money, or it's not the right time. I think about some of the things my mom did for me. I didn't have a father and I think she did some things to replace or what he'd have done if he'd been there.

I'm really trying to accentuate the positive, being a dad. She's old enough now where those personality traits we've had a chance to refine so that she'll make pretty good decisions in the future . . . I hope.

o   On Consistency & Solitude – Isaiah Daniels

Initially, I did not want to have kids because I felt like my childhood was miserable, but then, we had my daughter. I had a real hard time initially because I didn't know what a father was supposed to do. And then one day I said, "Well, Isaiah, you know, you can just start with: you can't treat your daughter the way you were treated." And so I got down on the floor.

Siobhan was a very active child; she had a strong personality, just like me. I said, "Ok, Siobhan, you want to play?" and she threw me on my back and sat on my chest and started pounding like "this is fun!" I said, "Oh my gosh, this girl's got a lot of spunk." We've been very close ever since.

I went out of my way to express my love for my daughter, no matter what happened. Now, I did have boundaries. I asked her why she didn't get a lot of spankings when she was a child. She said, "Well, Daddy, you always kept your word. If you said, if you do so-and-so, you're gonna' get blessed, I got blessed 100% of the time. But if you said if you do so-and-so you're going to whip my behind, I got whipped 100 times out of 100." She said, so she just sat there and figured out, "What kind of day do I want to have?" It's been one of the greatest experiences of my life having a child and loving that child.

Now I'm a grandparent. I'm actually more longsuffering with her from life's experiences; some things just aren't that serious. And, you made a mistake –big deal; we can fix mistakes. I still don't tolerate bad attitudes. But, if you make a mistake, and you didn't know, we can fix that. And part of that has come from seeing how the Lord deals with me and learning what real agape love is and loving by decision. I don't always do it right, but that's my intent. And I'm trying to deal with the finicky parts of my personality that sometimes just want to be left alone. I'm a loner by nature, so to have people around in my life, sometimes it's a lot of work for me.

o Only By God's Grace – Mike O'Coffey

When Selina got pregnant, I wasn't even a believer. I became a believer when she was eight months pregnant. I was just a gung ho' cop at the time, had been married three years and just excited to take the next step. I don't even know if I was thinking all that much about what it "meant." I know I was excited and scared – like I really didn't know what I was going to do. I knew I wanted to have more than the one child because I was an only child myself. And thought it would be fun to pass on things I knew. I don't know; it was just this "next-thing-to-do-after-being-married" kind of thing.

Of course, everything changed when I became a Christian. There was new meaning to life. After I became a believer, and that was before Abraham was born, then things got pretty important to me: to teach my son or my child the faith.

My wife was Jewish, so THE issue, when I became a believer was: how were we going to raise the child in a two-faith family? I sought out help from both pastors and rabbis. Both sides gave us at least one piece of similar advice: you need to pick ONE direction as parents to "go" in so that the kids don't feel like they're picking a parent when they are picking the religion. Then wait until the child gets older to expose them to both.

Those were some rocky days for us 'cause Selina didn't like that I was a Christian, and I was new at learning what it meant to be a Christian. I didn't understand the freedoms that I had in Christ, so I was probably a little bit rigid with the faith. But she did follow me in raising our kids in the Protestant Christian faith. And I took it pretty seriously. My primary inheritance that I was going to pass on to my children was the understanding of who Jesus Christ is. That probably still is the most overriding goal of my parenting. That's a lot of the reason why I continue to learn and study even now, so that I can give my children an accurate representation of who Christ is.

Unfortunately what I've learned being a Christian is that one of the main ways I teach my children about who God the Father, Jesus Christ, and the Holy Spirit are, is by clarifying that the Godhead is not always reflected in me. What they see in me is a lot of failure to reach standards. But God has made me very honest with them, that the behavior that they're seeing is not that of a man following Christ closely—that behavior was actually that of a man NOT following Christ. But please do not ascribe to Christ or God the Father the sinfulness you just saw me displaying.

Much of my fathering has been a lamenting over my inability to follow Christ as closely as I'd like. But I don't end there; I share with my children the joy of knowing the forgiveness and the belief that His Spirit is present there for new grace to come again. Gradually I grow, and I sin less in specific areas. But it's of premium importance to tell them the truth – "If I don't tell you this, then you will think that what I'm displaying is Christianity, and you will reject the faith. I would if I were you. But God will correct me." So much of my job is to make that distinction.

I mean, I'm pretty much God's representative to them, especially when they're young, right? My deepest fear, after I became a Christian, was always that I would drive my own children away from Christ. When I looked around, that's typically what I saw. So I'm probably ultra honest about my failings with my own kids. God's just made me repent before them many, many-a time.

I saw that behavior modeled throughout the text of the Bible – leaders putting their shortcomings out there; that's why they went to Christ or why they went to God. They needed help. And I figured, boy that's my way of boasting in my weaknesses that the power of Christ might rest on me. [2 Cor. 12:9] By example, my children, I hope, will learn to do the same.

I'd rather that they know the difficulty I have in following Him because they're going to face the same challenge. I also try more and more to have positive means to explain to them, so I take them with me when I'm out and about so that they can see me interacting kindly with people. I share with them how I try to handle situations (I would handle it in my flesh this way, but I don't think that's how God's calling me to do it, even though I really want to do it that way), so that they see the struggle. And they see how much I have to pray just to follow Christ in this world we live in.

Because I know that my own kids may judge the Father based on my behavior, it's significant that a result of my fathering is that the ultimate glory goes to God the Father. Therefore, I know it's important to do a better job of using more wisdom and discernment and be more loving and kind, even as I'm firm — even as I protect the family, and so forth, and to lead them into truth in the scriptures.

On the positive end, I do that by finding easier and easier ways to get them into the scriptures. Early on, I made it really tough for them. Bible study was laborious. I understood the importance of teaching my kids about Christ and how to live as a Christian in this world, but I really didn't know how to do it, and so I did things like saying "No" to a Christmas tree and to TV. I now understand my freedoms, so we now celebrate Christmas and when we do Bible studies they don't last an hour long — that's too much on a young kid. So I've really kind of lightened that up. Of course, that's from having learned from other men who are more mature in the faith and just growing in my own knowledge of the scriptures.

So a lot of my fathering is teaching them while they're sitting and while they're walking along the road, finding easier ways to get into the scriptures and asking, "Well, what do you think it's saying right here in the text?" Ok, "And if it's saying that, what does that mean for us?" Trying to be lighter about it. So I've gotten better and better at that. So now I have the kids read maybe 5 verses each. We ask a few questions and pray from the text. So they see how easy it is to understand the Bible. And they get kind of a more enjoyable, easy task. That's been the progression.

And now with the employment challenges I've had since I got hurt on the job, I've struggled to trust this God that I say I follow. And I have once again had to be on my knees a lot, praying before the kids. I don't know if this is a good thing or not. I share with them quite a bit of my fears and hurts, which I give to God to carry. I don't try to hide that. I don't feel like I gotta' put on a good face to make it look good. I figured that if I do that they're going to hit the real world and think, "Wow. What did my dad do to make it?" I mean, "Was he fakin' it?" And then I try to give glory to God when He comes through. And He comes through over and over and over again.

Some of the areas of life I feel like I'm weak in, because I didn't really do it with my father. For instance, I have an inability to teach the kids how to fix things . . . I'm not good at mechanics. My dad and I used to go hunting and fishing and riding motorcycles and I don't tend to do those kinds of things with my kids, especially since I got hurt. It does kind of worry me a little bit that I don't do that kind of stuff as much with them. But we do a little bit here and there. We travel around. And I just try and keep them with me. I participate in the home schooling. Try to make them feel safe. They know that I'm the one who'd protect them if something bad happens. I feel like it's important for the kids to have that sense of security. And they don't feel like they have to defend themselves. I want them to have a pretty innocent life and have me expose them to things at an age- appropriate level.

But I do make life a little unpredictable for them sometimes. We went to places like Shaker's Village in Lexington, Kentucky, east of where we lived in Louisville. We needed a little getaway. We took off for the day. And then I changed the plan and we stayed the night. That was the funny part. We rented a room. They were like, "Stay the night?" It was an old Pilgrim's kind of place.

But the kids were like, "We don't have any toothbrushes or change of clothes." They wouldn't do that kind of stuff.

I said, "C'mon, it's not going to kill us. We can sleep in our underwear."

And they were kinda' looking at me funny like, "Are you serious?"

Those are kinda' fun memories and we had a great time! 'Cause I want them to feel that they can kinda' roll with things in life. I don't want them to be scared. I'm more scared now than I used to be because I'm older, and I feel fragile. I have to pray past mountains of anxiety, but God comes through for me.

But for my children, I want them to avoid what I've seen in the Christian world where it's like once you get outside the Christian bubble, sometimes, you can't deal with other people. That is not to be feared. I'm thinking, Lord, I want my kids to be able to deal with anybody that You call 'em to deal with. So I feel like I need to expose them. Those are kinds of things that I think fathers tend to do more than the mothers – be a little less protective of what they're exposed to and then we talk about it. "Okay, what'd you think about this movie? What was the worldview?"

And then I try to give my kids confidence by saying things like, "I know you guys'll do fine out in the world. Look at how much the Lord has cared for us, despite different setbacks and things like that. I want you to remember that so you'll have confidence, too, when you're facing difficulties – to turn to the Lord. And He will carry you through." So I get to do a lot of that stuff with my kids. They seem pretty well-adjusted.

* * * * *

I am 100% in agreement with the final speech from the movie, "Courageous." I believe "that God desires for every father to courageously step up and do whatever it takes to be involved in the lives of his children.

But more than just being there or providing for them, he's to walk them through their young lives and be a visual representation of the character of God, their Father in Heaven. . . . He should model how to walk with integrity and treat others with respect, and should call out his children to become responsible men and women who live their lives for what matters in eternity."[15]

The world presents multiple challenges to fathers daily. Fathers don't hold all of the answers to mending our frayed society. We know that, in and of itself, fatherhood is no cure-all. In fact, even with your most earnest and noble efforts at being a model father, your children may still have unresolved development issues. Nevertheless, you should never neglect the opportunity, as a father, to unlock the God-given hopes and dreams within your children. "When they are grown, you hope that they look back on you as their hero, someone who shaped their life for good,"[16] like Carey Roberts did.

> *"Thank you, Dad, for being there. You were more than essential. You were a beacon of truthfulness, common sense, kindness, and silent courage."[17]*

While types of demands from the children change during a life-time, from a newborn baby to full grown adult, the need for fathering is ever-present. "Fathering is not a sprint; it is a marathon. Fathering isn't finished until a man is lying six feet under."[18]

SECOND CHAPTERS OF LIFE

"I didn't mean to mess up your life, or your mother's. And I know I don't deserve a second chance at being your father, but I'm asking for one anyway."
—Save the Last Dance

In this generation, there've been a lot of fathers who are drugged out, tripped out, abusers, rebellers, thieves, robbers, hateful . . . whatever you can think of. Will you still love him as Jesus does? Or will you focus on yourself and say look what he did to me? This can take a lot out of you, but in order for you to move onward and upward, you've got to come to the place where you start seeing your father, with all his mistakes and errors, in the spirit. See him as somebody who's maybe been beat up, maybe been attacked, and you love him and want to bring life to him – the same way that God looks at you, and sees how you've been beat up and done in. And with all the things you've done, God is still reaching to bring life out of you.[1]

o   The First Time – Giji

What was to become a trademark of my father's periodic visits happened in conjunction with his very first one – he was late! He was supposed to have arrived around 2 or 3pm. When he wasn't there by 4pm or so, I was so zapped by anxiety and the physical exertion of cleaning and cooking like a maniac that I fell asleep.

It must have been around 7pm that I heard a man's voice filtering through my subconscious. I had heard no knock or doorbell, nor had I heard anyone call my name to arouse me, so at first I wasn't sure if

I were awake or dreaming. As the voice gained volume and clarity, I realized "it must be MY FATHER"!

The excitement of seeing my father for the first time overpowered all predilections to impress; I neither washed my face nor combed my sleep worn hair before stumbling through partial awakeness into the living room to greet him. I can still see him smiling as I came around the corner out of my room and moving toward me to hug me. I don't remember why now, but I recall limiting the closeness of our first embrace.

I kinda' remember thinking this is all happening too fast! I held his elbows and stared, thinking, "Dang, he's handsome! Nice suit. My eyes look just like his! Now I see why Mommie says we have a "Dick Tracy" head. And we do have the same complexion!" I don't know how long I stood there with these private thoughts cascading through my mind.

I do remember that suddenly I was hit with a resurrected wave of anxiety and fear about how my mother would treat him. It seemed "so far, so good," but how long would this last? Would anything happen to disrupt this "dream come true"? She was amazingly calm, cool, and cordial–even warm. I'm not sure what I expected her to say or do, but it obviously wasn't any of the above. I was nervous and amazed all through dinner. But as the night waxed on, I relaxed and just received her acceptance as an unexpected blessing.

Around midnight, Mommie left us to continue our sharing that first night and, for the very first time, my father and I laughed, and talked, and played chess into the wee hours of the morning–memories that I will treasure forever.

For the next 17 years we had infrequent, but always rich, times that we spent together. In fact, the depth of our intimacy was uncanny to a lot of people. He often called me, "Babe." One day I came home from work and all of my roommates were looking at me funny and started asking to see the ring and why was I holding out on them. I was completely clueless. They then explained that a man with a deep voice had left me a message on the answering machine, who addressed me as "Babe." I was delighted, after listening, to let them know that it was my dad.

During my first visit to his home in Georgia, we went to the neighborhood grocery store. We're both very affectionate and often walked with our arms around one another. As we stood in front of the cashier, I began to feel the hot glare of disapproval at his having his arm around this woman –out in public, no less. Even though he tried to introduce me as his daughter, the woman had already made up her mind about the inappropriateness of our actions and spat out, "And how's your **wife**?" The real precious part? My father was so engrossed in having a fabulous time with his daughter that he was completely oblivious to the woman's not-so-subtle attitude of accusation.

o More Friend Than Father– Alex

I've kinda' learned to let the past go. I mean, you can never get back those years that were lost. He's my father but . . . to me he's more like a buddy—like a friend. I still missed that bonding that really only happens as a child. Even though he acknowledges me as a success and he's proud of me and what-not, it still comes off as more like a friend telling you, "You did good," – not like a father's affirmation. But I love him. And I can tell I love my dad. And I know without a doubt he loves me, too.

We talk about women, but I mean we don't talk about women. He would say something and I'd be like, "Okay." But I don't know if it's just me or if it's guys, in general, who haven't had their father around; I don't feel that comfortable talking to my dad about relationships, which is weird. But then again, I don't feel comfortable talking with my mom about it, either. Definitely not my uncle. So like friends, but not my family.

Like I never had "the sex talk," where your parents sit you down and tell you about the birds and the bees. I've been taught what NOT to do, but I haven't been walked through the process of this is what life is about, "Son, this is what a man does" – nothing like that. So I guess there's an unspoken sense of, I guess, "taboo" with certain things. They assume that we got that message. Like we'd watch a movie and something would show up on the screen, and it might be something that was inappropriate, and my mom would be like, "He shouldn't be doing that. You know what should be done, right?" But she wouldn't come out and have an open discussion about things.

One thing that concerns me about my father is that he's not a spiritual or Christian example. He's a really good guy. He's a good human being, but I can't look up to him for like godly advice. It's really strange, but I feel like that's something that should be there for a father and son. Because it's a very profound topic, and if you can't go to your dad, for that type of advice, to me it kind of like puts a limit on how far you can really go with that person.

The rest of my family back home is very Christian-oriented. I grew up in the church—not that that made a difference with me getting saved, but at least I had that environment there, so we grew up with certain values and what-not, which I definitely think served me better in life . . . so far.

But I do appreciate just having someone I can rely on. Because I'm not from here, but my dad's here, it's reassuring security-wise to know I have a family member that I can go to in the States, like if I need a place to stay or if I need a place to go for the holidays – I have that connection.

o   Adult Bonding– Fran

There was a time where as a teenager I really didn't think about going to visit my father or his family much. I always kept in touch with his sister who would come and pick me up; I always had a relationship with her that helped bridge the gap between me and my dad during those years when there was not much contact.

So as an adult, I could decide to go on my own, so I did go and visit his side of the family more. I can just remember the more I would come around, the more that I would show him kindness and love, the more he would respond. So it did continue, until we actually could have a good time together.

One of my fondest memories after we'd really begun building our relationship was when I was over at my aunt's house for some occasion—a birthday or something. And he and I were again, alone, in the family room watching TV. Actually the kids were watching "Shrek," and only he and I ended up being there watching it, and we're seeing all this adult humor. So we were laughing, kind of playing off of each other, looking at this movie. And it was just one of those times when it felt like we had always been close.

o   The Next Generation– Felecia

So, for my girls to go over and spend time with "Grandaddy," was a wonderful turn of events. I asked initially, "Ya'll call him "Grandaddy!?" – They were like, "Yeah!" and they just loved it! I felt like, "Finally, the piece of him that I didn't get, they'll get it." He'd take the girls and give me a breather because he and his wife loved kids, and they always enjoyed having somebody or their children at their house, either visiting or living there. It was never ever just him, my stepmom and their two kids.

And that was great until that one fateful weekend came: he said, "I'm on my way," and he never showed. I let it go. And he did it again. And I let it go. I'm one that believes that everyone deserves a second chance.

So the third time, I didn't let go. Because then I realized that was a pattern and that if it was ever going to be broken, then I'd have to be the one to break it. And I let him know, in no uncertain terms. Because we talked. Good, bad, or indifferent, we had that kind of relationship. Even when I was a little kid I could say to him whatever. And I had the freedom to do that without being fearful or intimidated. I didn't have that kind of relationship with my mother. And his other children didn't have that kind of relationship with him. I took it upon myself to be that way with him and he allowed it.

So I said to him, "You know, you did that to me. You made me wait. And I was happy to wait because it was you. But you will not do this to my children. You did it to me, but you will not do it to my children – your grandchildren—ever again. I would rather them not ever see you again than to see their disappointed faces for an entire weekend because you broke their hearts. You did it to me; you will not do it again." And from that point, that pattern was broken. And it was broken to the point that he came and got them and kept them for two months in the summer. In fact my girls said, "Mommie, we were gone so long, I thought you gave us away!" But that was his way of saying, "I'm sorry."

o New Revelation—Kellee

In October 2011, two weeks prior to our observance of Yom Kippur, I felt like the Holy Spirit told me to "Google" my father, which I had never done in 20 years. When I did, I read all this stuff about the case, the trials, and the evidence. I was taken aback by reading different articles on what had reportedly happened. I was shocked by things of which I was unaware as a child and was deeply saddened with the realization of all that my dad went through. With all of that, I just broke down and cried. It just really hit me.

Had somebody stepped up in the MTA and said, "Hey, you know, what, he has an alcohol issue, we need to go ahead and fire him, or do something—stop him from driving these trains," it would have never happened. And because of the high-profile incident, they NOW have started doing random drug screens and testings and stopped all these people who were riding around with drugs and alcohol in their system driving trains. It just so happened that my father was made the example. Then they wound up letting a lot of people go after what had happened.

Apparently, he'd skipped the first stop on the train, and the conductor said something to him. He apologized and said, "It won't happen again," but it did. The third time it happened is when the train crashed and five people died. He had issues with alcohol before, and it was just a big 'ole mess.

At the trial, in his remorse, my father said he wished it had been him who'd died instead of the other people. They were trying to get him on murder two, for depraved indifference. But instead, he was found guilty of manslaughter—negligent homicide. What prompted me to share my testimony was that I was thankful because he could have been put away for life, instead of five to 15, for which he served 10 years and five years parole. So it could have been that I would never have seen my father again outside the walls of a jail cell.

When all of that hit me, I was just so thankful. It has taken me some years, but God took me back to show me things I should be thankful for. We see things on a daily basis, but He had this moment where He just took me back, to periods where I didn't know Him. It was like, "Be thankful for what I did 20 years ago. You didn't know Me, but now you do, so I can show you what all I did." So it was a huge burden lifted.

Of course, I wrote a letter to my dad with the testimony that I had read at church. He feels like it can't be everything the reports say. And, it's true, that reporters will ad lib, but I think I pretty much got the gist of it. Of course, the people whose family members died wanted to see my dad go away for a long time. So they were upset and were always at the trials.

I watch Law & Order and all these shows where you see a person on trial and I never thought about it that my father went through that; it never even crossed my mind. I don't know – I was shielded. It never crossed my mind that he was in a court room for a year while awaiting a verdict—that my father was in jail for a year before the court even pronounced the final sentencing.

Ironically, when I contacted my brother and told him, "Hey, Google Dad." He said, "Yeah, I did it earlier this year." The same year.

I remember my mom's friend was working at the jail and he'd called and let us know the day that my father was going to be getting out of jail. Then my dad went to a half-way house for five years on probation. I saw him a couple of times, but he had to have passes and had to be back at the house by a certain time. But I was really happy that he was getting out.

My dad and I have a great relationship—even though he can be stubborn or, I should say, may not really listen or take a advice from a lot of people. But our relationship is one where I have the opportunity to minister to my dad a lot. He takes it and dwells on it and meditates on it. He knows a lot of Word; he knows that God is calling him to do something. He just needs to stop and put the bottle down long enough and be the man of his household in order to do so.

We have a father-daughter relationship, but it's also like a friendship. Because I don't just talk to him like, "Hey Dad, how ya' doin'?" I talk to him like, "Look, what are you doing? You don't need to be in this place. You need to man-up and do this. God wants you to do that." He loves that.

I wrote him this letter once about forgiveness. I talked about how I forgave him and stuff like that. This was back when he was in one of his programs, like AA. He read the letter out loud, and everybody was in tears. He carries the letter around with him to this day as encouragement. I didn't even know until this past Christmas, and we were taking pictures, and it was in his bag. He said, "I carry this around every day."

The biggest thing is that we have a great friendship, where I can talk with him and be honest with him and he can receive it. He's not like, "Who are you? You're my daughter. You don't know what you're talking about. I've known God longer than you." It's not like one of those. He respects me. He respects my walk. And he respects what I have to say.

o The Castle Move—Mike

When I went to college, I had my own life. I really wasn't engaged with my dad. The big change in our relationship has occurred within the last five years.

I got hurt in 2001 with my neck injury; until then, I had been pretty strong and been able to do what I wanted to do. After getting injured, I didn't play with the kids, and I was cranky a lot of times. So I was still searching for other fathers, at this point, mostly men I had met in the Amway business. But there, too, the men that I looked up to quickly disappointed me when I found they weren't living up to the scriptures. They presented themselves as God-fearing Christian men, so I wanted to follow them.

My stepfather, Patrick, did teach me how to fight for the underdog. It took me a while to recognize the misuse of the scriptures by men I looked up to and trusted as fathers. But once I learned these men were using the scriptures to dominate people and take advantage of weaker people, I had no problem standing up to that. I wasn't going to cave to that. So I was still hunting for men who I thought knew more than me spiritually. As a result, I wasn't inclined to go back to Patrick—it wasn't like he had a strong theological background.

With the physical limitations and resulting employment challenges I faced, even after having become an elder in the church, I believed that I was failing in life and not able to live up to the performance standards I'd set for myself. When I talked to my mom about it, she was just encouraging about it. "It'll be okay. Praise Jesus. Praise Jesus." I felt like, "This isn't helping." She hadn't walked the road that my dad had walked – he'd failed too.

So this natural gravitation happened to want to hear from my dad about how he'd handled different struggles. He was always the kind of man who would fight for things. He was proud of me because the battles I fought for righteousness among the eldership at my church cost me and my family a lot; I fought fights that costs me dearly—friends, advancement. The cost was born by my wife and children. There are some regrets I have about that now, and wonder if it mirrors what my dad did.

My dad also had back problems. His answer was my mother's herbal medicine and acupuncture. There were a lot of similarities, including job loss because of my injury. He also did caution me in my over-involvement with the church. Even though I was talking to him, it wasn't like I had this respect for my dad. The discounting of my dad earlier in my life caused me to discount him again. I wish I hadn't this time; he was right.

When I was younger I'd put pressure on my dad to take care of my mom better. Then when I started feeling the pressure—to be kind to my own wife and my own kids—I began to empathize with my father. Who did I think I was that I thought I could advise him on how to be a husband?

My mom knew her Bible at that time much better than my dad, but I had a strong resistance to that. I didn't want to be comforted by my mom anymore. When I was younger, they had a battle over whether I should work. My mom won. That decision led to a lack of confidence in me – where I needed the environment to be taken care of in order for me to succeed. I knew that her coddling wasn't going to help me deal with the hurdles I needed to overcome. I was never disrespectful to my mom. She is a wise woman, and she did not resist as she saw me pulling away from her and going to my dad.

I needed someone to vent to who was outside the system, so that's when the pendulum swung to frequent communication with my dad. I think that period of being engaged in warfare inside my church family was one of the most painful seasons of my life. I felt like I had gone through multiple divorces. I think there was a period of about three years where I talked with my dad almost every day– and it was just out of anxiety. He didn't always know what to say, but it was nice to be able to talk to my dad. He might just say, "Yeah, I know what that's like." And I know he was praying for me.

My dad had offered a lot of warnings about those men– far before I ever saw it– but I didn't want to listen to him. I didn't think that was possible that what he saw about these men were using me like he said— we were fellow elders. Had I had more traction with my dad earlier, I would have been inclined to listen to him and avoid so much pain and misery. I'm not blaming my dad, but there's this sense of regret. By then I was broken and brittle and unable to bounce back.

I literally tried to abandon the Christian faith because I was so disappointed by the church, and God's allowing me to take my gifts and have them abused by my fathers in the faith, at a time I was unable to trust my earthly father. Jesus Christ was not satisfying enough for me to delight in following the combination of pain, loss of friends, loss of job—so then I found myself in a fight with my Heavenly Father. Concepts of God's sovereignty sounded so hallowed to me. During that time, I still felt I needed to share with my dad. By this time, my dad was reading his Bible faithfully and we were having more scripturally relevant conversations.

I went from loving to spend time in the Word, to almost dreading it. But it was like I could not stop believing the Lord—I just didn't like it. And I didn't like the Church. I had to remember that the Church is the Lord's bride and the bridegroom's responsibility is to care for her.

All that pulled me away from emotional closeness with my family —you get in a big enough fight and it takes enough out of you. And I'm still working through the restoration of some of that loss. But my closeness with my dad is fruit that has remained. To this day, it's hardly more than two or three days go by that I don't talk to my dad.

Cut From the Same Cloth

"And where does the acorn fall? . . . He's his daddy's boy."
—The Blind Side

○ Very Much My Father's Child – Giji

"Daddy" rolled off my tongue effortlessly, even though I never had practiced. And to me, he was definitely "Daddy" and not "Dad," which is what my brothers call him. The more we talked, the more pieces of my own idiosyncratic puzzle fell into place. Our writing styles were very similar–his a bit more philosophical and poetic. We both had this strange fascination about the subject of death. I finally had some clue as to my "street-wise" proclivities, despite having been reared by my reserved, protective mother.

Mommie was the classical and spiritual musician. Daddy and I preferred jazz. The storyteller, the sensitive intervener, a rescuer of the wayward, and the passionate orator were all parts of my design that mirrored Robert Deadwyler's. So I discovered that, although Kha Dennard had left an indelible print of herself on me in terms of physical appearance and mannerisms, in a lot of ways, I am very much my father's child.

My dad had a sort of "criminal" side—very different from my mother, who was often rather naïve and sheltered. I inherited my father's street sense but, because I didn't know him, often wondered "how'd I end up being **this** woman's child?" When I met my father, all of that made sense. But even in high school, I led very "007" lives – one was as my mother's child, the other was as my father's child.

Echoing my sentiments, Daddy wrote just before I graduated from law school: "I need your love; I need our relationship. God gave you to me so we can be there for each other at whatever needed time. We must be together—in so many ways, we're very much alike."

I was also twice-destined to be a "pk." Not only was my biological father a fervent minister of the gospel, but the very one who has remained a steadfast "Dad" in my life is also an elder in ministry. Rev. Ripley came back into my life during my undergraduate days – after Daddy had an opportunity to fill his own shoes – and remains an anchor of the soul for me to this day.

o   The Good & the Bad– Fran

Characteristics that my father and I share? Yes, lots! And my mom is quick to tell me that. One of the things was anger. Before I got saved I used to be very angry. And my dad, he was kind of an angry drunk. When he would get intoxicated, I could see things would set him off. That's one thing, but we also share several little idiosyncrasies, such as, being particular about where things are, where we leave them, and where we want them left.

Personality-wise though, even though he was a very angry man at times, he was very giving. He really cared about people, and a lot of people knew him. I mean before and after he passed, I realized he had touched so many people. He knew a lot of people. He would actually give advice to a lot of the young guys in the neighborhood who were going the wrong way. It was like he always had this knack for relating to people. Which I think might have been something that frustrated him because one of the people he loved and cared about most he couldn't reach – which was me. But in the sense, too, that I care a lot about people and reach out a lot to people; I saw that side of my father reflected in me.

My mom was quick to tell me, especially after she and my dad had started dating again, about my similarities with my father. He would spend a lot more time at her house and stuff. She was frequently heard saying, "Oh. Now I know where you get some of that stuff from. You're just like your father."

o   Common Ground– Alex

It's so strange that after that separation for so long and then reconnecting, you realize that you have so much in common. Like our sense of humor, for one – the things we laugh at. What we like to eat;

we both love food. I guess, guy stuff, in general, you could say . . . like electronics, games, and movies.

o Twins– Felecia

I'm his twin. I look just like him. And we had the same kind of humor. I think a lot of the brunt that I got as a kid from my Mom was because I look so much like him. And she took it out on me. All those feelings she had for him . . . I got that. But it's okay.

o Fellow Roadrunners—Perry Fuller

What do we have in common? I think Jasmine's pretty easy-going; I think I am. I think she gets along with a wide spectrum of different kinds of personalities of people. I think I can see she's gonna' be a giver, and I think she got that from me and Margot. And I think she can be aggressive and assertive, and I definitely think she got that more from me than Margot. I think she got the outgoing part from me and getting bored with things easily—which is good and bad. But at least I think she's expressing it better than I did. I was caught up into the girls and sports; she more is pursuing her studies and the clothes. The guy is there, but at least—as far as I know– she's being true to who she is Christian-wise. I know she got that part about always being on the go from me; that child never sits still. I was like that pretty much when I was younger.

o Like Father, Like Husband?–Kellee

We both talk a lot. That's one thing my mom always used to say. We're both caring and loving. We're very giving people—like we'll give our last in order for the next person to have what they need. If someone needs a place to stay, they've always had a room. For some reason, my dad's nice hand-writing and the drawing skipped over me – that went to my brother. I started to play the drums when I was younger because my dad and my mom were in a band, but I didn't keep up with it. That's another thing – if he weren't locked up, I think I would have kept up with the drums.

It's kinda' funny because I think my husband and my dad have a lot of common characteristics. My grandmother was even telling my mom over Christmas that my mother and I have similar tastes. It's interesting how that happened because I wasn't around my dad. So to put me with a man who has similar characteristics as my father was deep. They usually say when a woman's around her father, she usually marries the same type of guy, but I wasn't really around him. When you see my father and my husband together, it's just hilarious.

THE ETERNAL CONTEXT

"I set out on a narrow way many years ago. Hoping I would find true love along the broken road. . . . I couldn't see how every sign pointed straight to You. Every long lost dream led me to where You are. Others who broke my heart, they were just northern stars pointing me on my way into Your loving arms. . . . It's all part of a grander plan that is coming true."

—Rascal Flatts, "Bless the Broken Road"

o Who's Yo' Daddy Now?

Several years ago, the Lord revealed a 5-part comparison between common earthly father types and the contrasting character of the Heavenly Father to Assistant Pastor Vonda Pipkin of ReJOYce in Jesus Ministries. She believes that one of the things hanging up the body of Christ from perceiving God's love and getting the revelation of His love for us is because of our relationship with our parents in the past – whoever your authority figure was. Whether it was a father, a mother, an uncle, a grandparent –often times it painted a picture for us of what we think the Heavenly Father's like. She admonishes us to renew our minds to what God is truly like – to get rid of misconceptions about God.

- *The Absent Father* – He just wasn't around. Vonda, herself, had the absent father. Her father lived in Hampton, VA, her mother lived in Manassas, and they divorced when she was around three years old. So the whole idea of growing up with a daddy, sitting in his lap and pulling his beard is foreign to her.

Likewise, if you didn't have a relationship with your earthly father, when you get saved, you don't know what it's like to sit in the Heavenly Father's lap.

Mothers will do what they need to do, but a mother can't be a daddy – it's just not in them. They may provide and try to do the things that a dad may do, but they cannot take the place of a dad. The Lord's ultimate plan was for the two parts to come together. The focus of the mother tends to be more temporal, nurturing us for the "now." The man typically is the parent pushing you for the future. When the father's not there, you often don't have that person in your life who says, "Oh get up, you'll be okay." Then, all of a sudden, you run into God the Father, and you don't know that stern hand.

If your father wasn't there, there's something we still have to learn about the Heavenly Father. The Lord told Vonda, "I'm not like your father, the absent father. **I am the accessible Father.**" He's given us access to the throne of grace. "Boldly come before My throne of grace that you may find grace to help in time of need." [Heb. 4:16] I'm always there. You don't ever have to worry that I'll be there one day and gone the next." In Heb. 13, God says, "I'll never leave you or forsake you." In other versions it says, "I will never give you up nor ever at all desert you." "I will never forsake you, nor will I ever abandon you."

You have to meditate on the Heavenly Father's words and stop ruminating about what your earthly father was like. Even if it's subconscious, it will keep you from experiencing God's love if you don't replace your thoughts with the realization that God's not going to leave you. There may be times that He will pull back the "warm fuzzies" that sometimes accompany His presence, so that you will stay in faith and not walk by feelings, but that doesn't mean He has abandoned you. In those times, you will have to hold fast to the Word.

Furthermore, if you grew up thinking, if you want something done, you have to do it yourself, because your father wasn't there to take care of things, it can be very difficult for you to depend on the Lord. You'll have a tendency to think God doesn't move fast enough. But you have to learn to trust and rely on Him. God wants you to seek Him and let Him direct your steps.

- *The Apathetic Father* – Perhaps your father was there, but he showed no emotion. The word apathy means "no passion," so he didn't have a passion for anything you were involved in. He was reading the newspaper or watching the TV most of the time. And he didn't seem that he was interested in the little details that you were interested in.

  Frequently, if you had a father who was like that, you may tend to think that the Heavenly Father doesn't care about details. So then the times that you need to go and talk to the Father about the little everyday things in life, you tend to draw back and think, "Oh God doesn't want to hear that. Kids are dying over in Bosnia, why would God want to hear about my little promotion or the 10 pounds I gained over the holidays? Why would God care about something like this?" But see, God says, "**I care about you affectionately.**" I Pet 5:7(AMP) "Casting the whole of your care, all your anxieties, all of your worries, all of your concerns, once and for all on Him for He cares for you affectionately and cares about you watchfully." God's love for you is passionate! God loves us because we're His – not because of what we do or don't do.

- *The Authoritative Father* – Some of us had fathers who just cracked the whip. "You will submit in this household. No questions asked." Some had fathers to whom you dared not ever talk back. There is a right and a wrong way to ask questions. You don't have to know everything before you obey, but get understanding along the way. When you become a parent, whatever you came up under, you will often mimic yourself. **God is the admonishing Father.** Admonish means to counsel, to warn, and to advise. He is the Author and Finisher of your faith, so "there are times He's going to tell you things you need to do, but you can talk to Him." Although He has authority, God is not a controlling dictator or tyrant who will force His will or counsel upon us.

- *The Abusive Father* – Abuse means "abnormal use." Abuse is where people don't know what something is there for so they use it for the wrong reason or in the wrong way. The very person to whom you looked for care and protection took something away from you because he didn't understand the purpose of a child. Even in disciplining a child, there's a place where you can feel that the Holy Spirit says, "Alright, you made the point. Don't hit him anymore; he got the message." And there's a place where you can spank too many times or too long or too hard and it stops being discipline and it turns into abuse. You need to be careful – you don't want to destroy the child's spirit. You don't own your children; you're stewards of them, but God is the owner. And God has allowed that child to be raised up in your household for a season, and you're going to stand before Him and be accountable for what you did with that child. An abusive father, often causes his children to think that the Heavenly Father is also out to abuse them. So when God brings discipline in our lives, we perceive that as "God's mad at me; He wants to hurt me." In fact, we think sometimes that God actually somewhat enjoys seeing us suffer. In actuality, if you discipline children correctly, in the pattern God sets forth in the Bible, while they will learn that there may be a corresponding pain resulting from disobedience, they also will be affirmed in their value and in your love for them.

God said, "I am not an abusive father." **He is our attentive Father.** He is attentive to everything that His children go through. James 1:17 says that "every good gift and every perfect gift is from above and comes down from the Father of light, with whom there is no variableness neither shadow of turning." God showed Vonda that no matter which direction He turns, He only casts light on the earth. Anything God allows in your life, it's because there's something good He wants to do in you. He says that His thoughts toward us are good and they're not evil, to give you an expected end, to give you a future and a hope. [Jer. 29:11] Vonda said she meditates on Romans 8:28 all the time, which says, "All things work together for good for them who love God and are the called according to His purpose" – even when she's going through challenging things. Especially in the midst of suffering, you have to know that God doesn't have any evil intentions toward you and that, in the end, He expects you to be victorious and come out like gold!

- *The Accusing Father* – If he was present, this is most likely the type of father he was. He meant well, but his approach wasn't ideal. In order to get you to behave correctly, he would reward the good and then he would reject you if you did wrong. He thought that was going to provoke you to do a better job. So many of us became performance oriented as a result. So even in the body of Christ, there are people all over the church who don't know how to "be still and know that He is God." [Psalm 46:10] Something resides in people which makes them think if they're not performing, then God is mad at them. It's because, as a child, you learned that "love is conditional. Love is based on what I do and what I don't do." So then when you accepted the Lord, all you did was change the position. It's fine to want to do the work of the church and occupy until He comes, but if your motivation is "this is how I'm going to get love from God," you've missed the point. God wants us to know that that love that He has for us is unconditional. He loves you just like you are already.

God says He is not the accusing father, **He is the accepting Father.** Luke 15 tells the story of the prodigal son. When we walk away from God, like this son, we are acting temporarily insane, or throwing away our inheritance. The father's response to his son's return is a picture of what God the Father is like.

"When the father finally reaches him, he doesn't make him grovel in the dirt. He doesn't question him to make sure he's learned his lesson. And he doesn't lecture him: 'Look at you, you're a disgrace' . . . 'I knew when the money ran out that you'd come crawling back' . . . 'You can come home, but only on one condition'. The father says none of those things."[1]

The parable Jesus shares not only draws poignant imagery of the attributes each earthly body was intended to embody – tenderness, compassion, understanding, and demonstrative love, but "cracks the door to heaven, ever so slightly, to reveal his own Father."[2]

Even when you are in a messed up state, God says, "I'm looking for you a great way off." God is sitting there waiting for you to come back. And the moment that you turn around – the second that you make that decision that "Lord, I don't want to keep living like this; what am I doing?" – He will have compassion for you and He will run to meet you where you are, passionately display His love and affection for you, clothe you in His very own righteousness – His **best** robe –, demonstrate his possession of you as His child, and celebrate and rejoice with you and over you because of your return home to your Father.

You have to be able to envision that picture so you can stop running from God – you'll stop running in the opposite direction. You'll run **in** His direction because you know He's not trying to hurt you; He's not trying to destroy you.

You need to renounce any wrong conceptions of God. If you maintain any of these false images of God, He wants to lift them from you so that you can come into His presence more deeply. God wants you to get to that place where you can have a passionate relationship with Him.[3]

*   *   *   *   *

"God is the model father. [T]he original, the standard of effective fatherhood [*is*] God Himself." He is a tender Father who invites us to address Him as "Abba," which means, "Daddy." [Rom. 8:15; Gal. 4:6] He is a listening Father who bids us to approach Him as "our Father in heaven." [Matt. 3:17] He is a giving Father who gives good gifts to His children. [Matt. 7:11] Therefore, if any man wants to become a good and effective father, the standard – the model—is God the Father.[4]

The key to this "Father Connection," as Josh McDowell calls it, is "the realization that God the Father is not only the incomparable *model* of effective fatherhood, He is the indispensable *resource* for becoming the father you long to be." The secret to superior fatherhood is not mere imitation or emulation – it requires association with the Creator of the concept. "It isn't about knowing how; it's about knowing Who!"[5]

Dr. Leman believes that "the presence of God is the most rewarding thing you can give a daughter," in the form of a "real relationship in which a child grows up knowing she is loved and watched over by her Father in Heaven." He believes that if parents can give kids a "really neat family" and a love for God, everything else will fall into place for them. "They'll make wise choices. They'll hang around the right people. They'll become the people God created them to be, and others will ask them, 'How can I get what you have'?"[6]

"[I]n the early years your daughters will directly connect you with God." Many parents have reported of toddlers "praying" to Daddy. When you demonstrate your love and commitment to your child by fervent and consistent immersion in her day-to-day activities, she will learn that her Heavenly Father is equally concerned about all areas of her life. "[T]here is no better inheritance that you can give your daughter [or son] than the inheritance of faith," and no better way to cultivate it than by being an involved father who loves the Lord.[7]

Even as they mature and begin to see more of their father's faults and certainly no longer think of him as all-powerful and all-knowing..., they're going to pick up how this man relates to the Creator of the universe. That's why prayer should "be a normal response to life, not an artificial stimulant that you inject into the family life in times of tragedy or stress."[8]

By virtue of the father's position in the home, he also represents authority to his children. How they "model and handle that authority will greatly influence how our [sons and] daughters learn to submit to God's authority.[9]

Whether the father or the child, if you've accepted Jesus Christ as your personal Lord and Savior, you're actually the offspring of the Living God! If you really see yourselves the way God, the Father, sees you – the one Who sent His Son to die for you, who's kept you alive all these years, and who knows the plans for a hope and a future that He has for you [Jer. 29:11] – you will readily embrace His perfect Father love for you, personally.

o 20/20 Vision – Bobby Deadwyler

But for both of us, the REAL reunion had taken place years before . . .

You see, in previous years, I lived on the corner of "Diabolical and Dangerous Avenues." I followed Satan around his sights of gaiety and false laughter. "Man," I was saying, "I'm on top of the world! I'm the King of the Players—I've got all these beautiful babes providing me with my every desire!" I was travelling full speed toward prison and hell in the vehicle of damnation, which was running off Satan's fuel of pride, lust, greed, and fleshly addictions, until the mercy of God pulled me over and gave me a warning!

Even though I had accepted the ticket, I had no intention of altering my diabolical lifestyle. But while sitting in my prison cell, I often noticed a note that someone had dropped on my bed. It was another one of those letters from Ted, a fellow inmate who'd accepted God's salvation while on death row, telling me again that God cares for me even if I don't care for Him! I got fed up with him and all that constant Jesus talk, and I threatened to break his jaw when we went out into the yard.

I didn't like any of those hymn singing, evangelical-minded ambassadors, and I insulted them every time they were in my presence. So, once and for all, I was planning to put my fist into Ted's head. All of the fellows in the line were walking fast to get to the yard to see the action! I rushed into the yard filled with hostility, and . . .

I couldn't explain it then, but I know now why I was unable to lift my arms to strike him. God dispatched an angel of protection to stand in front of Ted! I trembled inside while the fellows were laughing and making derogatory statements about my being "chicken." However, glory to God! On May 9, 1959, in my prison cell, I repented of my sins and begged God to save me like He saved Ted!

I had discovered that "there is a way that seemeth right to a man, but the end thereof is the way of death." [Prov. 14:14; 16:25]

o Full Circle – Giji

My mother, brother, and I had gone to church, of some sort, almost every Sunday for the first eight years of my life. Attendance was less frequent for a season after that. When I was about 12, my mom and I were attending Grace Episcopal Church in West Palm Beach, Florida. There were very few kids my age in the church, and like many other child churchgoers, I generally found the experience unrelatable.

Periodically, they would have special panels dealing with timely and relevant issues, and I even remember a performance of pieces from "Godspell" being done one Sunday, but overall, I was just there. But, for as long as I could remember, I had been very curious about God and spiritual things, especially the things my great-grandmother had shared before she finished her course and went Home to be with Jesus.

The Apostle's Creed was recited, from memory, every Sunday at Grace Episcopal. One morning, for the first time, I received it as true and really believed, and a conversion had taken place–just like it says in Romans 10:9-10! There was no fanfare, no invitation, no tarrying at the altar, but a change had taken place on the inside; there was a joy and excitement I had not known before – a hunger to know more about this Jesus Christ, Son of God, Savior. I was not familiar with the terms "saved" or "born-again," and yet, that morning, I became numbered among them.

My hunger for the things of God led me to a decision to become confirmed in that church. I can still remember the cover of the booklet, simply called *Jesus*, where I first learned about having a personal relationship with the Lord. I enjoyed it so much, in fact, that I tried to persuade the priests to allow me to go through the classes a second time– just for fun.

Unfortunately, my newfound revelation began to be short-circuited as we moved to different cities throughout the state over the next several years, never really settling in a church–at least not one where that spark was continually getting ignited. So, I started drifting farther and farther from the One True God, and getting deeper and deeper into the occult, eastern religion and mysticism, and generally hedonistic living. Then a strange thing happened my sophomore year in college.

My brother Dana, with whom I had grown up and who, for a short while, had known my father as "half-a-daddy," had given me this book called *The Autobiography of a Yogi*. I began to notice that so many spiritual teachers compared their philosophies to things Jesus had said–even the commentaries in the *Bhagavad-Gita*. It was at that point that I decided I really wanted to know for myself what Jesus had said. For the first time, I went and bought my very own Bible. I knew from that day forward that, there, I would find the truth I sought and never again would I have a need for any other "master."

My last two years of college I attended church regularly, but my life was not really the testimony of a disciple of Christ. I didn't really know how to turn from my life of immorality until the spring of 1984 when I attended a Bible study of ReJOYce in Jesus Ministries at Stanford University. I didn't know these people, but I knew the truth when I heard it. Three weeks later, I rededicated my life to the Lord, received the baptism of the Holy Spirit, and have continued in a radical conversion ever since.

And that's where I was presented my spiritual father of the last 28 years—Pastor Chester C. Pipkin, Jr. Whether from the pulpit, in a rap session, on a conference call, or over a card game, I can depend on him to be a rock solid shepherd guiding me through the mountain crags and the green pastures of this faith walk, with an unswerving truth, compassion, sincerity, faithfulness, and fatherly love.

I have no doubt that the circuitous spiritual path I took was, inevitably, ordered by the Lord, and that it commenced with an extremely significant act by my earthly father before he knew me. Suspecting that my mother had become pregnant on their honeymoon, very much like Hannah, my father prayed over me and dedicated me to the Lord while I was, yet, in my mother's womb. I am truly honored to carry that mantle of service to the Lord.

o The Short Version – Alex

How I got saved is a really long story. I could sit here and tell you that for two days. But trying to keep it in context – I told you how I grew up with all these insecurities, like an inferiority complex. I think the turning point was after I had my first real meaningful relationship with a girl. You look for certain ways to be affirmed. And I was dumped. I was really depressed, felt really low and down and what-not. I was invited by a friend in church to go to this all night prayer meeting. I was pretty active in the youth group, so I had friends in church. And that night, that night that I did get saved—that was the turning point for me as a person.

Not just like the act of getting saved. All those inferiority complexes, all those hang-ups, all those grudges, all that stuff was gone. I really see how people who get saved say, "I felt lighter, I felt like a new person." I can say that at that point in time, I completely changed. I felt like reading the Bible and seeing who God was and seeing that He called me His son—just the things that He expected of me as His lineage. That all the hang-ups and complexes I had were just false. It was like a psychological awakening, you could say.

I suddenly felt there was no reason to feel at a disadvantage. In fact, I had an advantage—I shouldn't feel inferior, I should have the most confidence in the world. Because the God of the universe, the King of kings, is saying to me "you're a prince; you're a part of Me." I think that really changed my outlook on a lot of things . . . how I interacted with people. I started branching out. I became really sociable. The way

I dealt with my family – I started to see things in my mom that I could really appreciate now. I think that brought us closer together.

I really felt like I was a different person and I started to explore that in my walk with Christ after I got saved. I read the scriptures and started seeing these different attributes of Christ and Him saying that these attributes are things that you should be doing and being even more. It was kind of like schooling; those things that I missed with my biological dad I was being ushered into through the Word. How to interact with people. How to view yourself. Going for like job applications, school applications, scholarship applications – having that sense of faith that it is going to work out.

I have the confidence to take what I set my eyes on in the world because He said it's fine. I just have to pray for it with supplication and do it. I really feel like that was the father that I should have had, and I'm really grateful for that.

o   Glad It Wasn't Too Late – Fran

I could not have had any idea that my father would die suddenly, and that I would not have seen him nor heard from him for a month or two – there were no words between us right before he passed away. I just got the call in the middle of the night saying your father just passed away. And when I went there where he was, there was nothing.

What gave me peace was I had reconciled with him, and I had made it a point whenever I ended a conversation with him, whenever I parted company with him, I always told him I loved him. Especially on the phone . . . He never wanted me to call him "Dad" or "my dad." I think he felt awkward because he didn't feel worthy to be called my dad after all those years of what we went through. But I had no regrets because I knew that the last thing I said to him was, "I love you."

Reconciling with my dad really started with how I had to reconcile with my mom. My mom had a drug problem which took our whole family into this downward spiral. Because of my perception, I always questioned, "Why'd she do this to us?" And when I got saved for real, I started looking at how God needed to change me and not just how He needed to change somebody else. The Lord had to show me, "Fran, you're okay. You found Me; I found you. You're walkin'. You're saved.

You're fine." He said, "Your mom is the one who really needs the help, not you." In the way I thought I needed the help.

And He showed me that she wasn't intentionally trying to do what she was doing to us. I got the chance to sit in the car (the same car from which the battery had been stolen) with my mom and the Lord led us into this discussion and I basically told her how I felt. That the one thing I could never understand is "Why would you do this to us?" She basically said, "I didn't realize what I was doing to you kids." That was the turning point.

When my mom and I reconciled, then the Lord started showing me things about my dad. I could see Jesus as my Savior. I could even relate and see Jesus as my husband. There was too much hurt there when I thought about "father." And He said, "You have a hard time seeing Me as Father, and relating to me as Father." After He began to speak that, He said he needed to show me some things about my perception of my earthly father and heal some things before I could truly see Him as God, the Father – my Father.

So, that was how my conversion and the Lord's transforming me launched me into my reunion –I like to say reconciliation– with my earthly father.

o Let It Go – Felecia

I'm the type of person who, as far as I'm concerned, I let stuff go. I don't dwell, I don't hold grudges; I just move on. While I've been like that all my life, I find that, now that I have a relationship with the Lord, the reasoning and the rationale is different. Before I knew Christ, I moved on because it was too painful not to. But, in a relationship with Christ, I move on because it's the godly thing to do – to not harbor unforgiveness. Because there's a scripture tied to that: so as we forgive others here on earth, so shall our Father in heaven forgive us. [Mark 11:26] So forgiveness has been a sort of central point, both inside of the Lord and outside of the Lord. And sometimes we move in a way that draws us to God and we don't know why.

o Antidote to Rejection – Isaiah

Because of rejection, and because I wanted to fit in so badly, I started joining the people who liked to get high. I wanted to be accepted by people, and this group would always accept any newcomer to the crowd.

So, through a series of very, very poor choices, I wound up flunking out of UC Santa Barbara. I went to Howard for a year. Now I should not have transferred, but I transferred to UC Santa Barbara. My father wanted me closer. I absolutely hated Santa Barbara, and so I decided to move to Hawaii.

When I moved to Hawaii, my addictive habits got worse, not better. All I can describe is this incredible draw inside of me that was like, "Ok, Isaiah, you have to move, you have to get to Los Angeles!" I was living on Maui in 1977 and what I was trying to do there was to start a business and start buying some land. Now if I'd done that, I'd be a multi-millionaire by now; that was another one of my life's dreams – to be a millionaire.

I used to keep a journal. While I was still in Hawaii, this co-worker came up to me one day and handed me a memo. It said: "From God to Isaiah, regarding drifting." And "drifting" had been the title of my journal the day before. And she had Psalm 100 in it. I ran after her and I said, "Where'd you get this?" She said, "Isaiah, I always do what God tells me to do." And she walked away. That's when I knew that maybe there was a God.

But I wound up coming back to L.A., and I hated L.A. By the time I got here, I was smoking two packs of cigarettes a day, I was a full-blown alcoholic, and I was doing drugs on a regular basis. And in fact, there was a three-year period of my life where I wasn't sober **any** one day. I was living with them, but I absolutely hated my parents, and I just wanted to move out. I didn't care where I went; I just didn't want to be around them.

When I moved out, though, I was financing a drug operation, where a friend of mine from childhood and I were selling drugs. We had some connections with some people in Hawaii, and we were bringing them over state-side and selling them.

It got to the point where I was drinking really heavily. At first I would go to bars. But eventually, I would just come home from work and drink a fifth of Tanqueray until I passed out. Then I'd wake up, smoke a joint, and go to work the next day. Well, they used to have this list on TV. You might be an alcoholic if . . . And they named these 10 things. Well, I had 7 of the 10. So I thought, "I might be an alcoholic."

I ran across a childhood friend of mine who was a member of ReJOYce in Jesus Ministries at a time I was probably at my lowest. I shared with him my life story. And at that time, I was planning the murder of my drug partner because he'd stolen some money and some drugs for a woman who didn't love him. I felt like I had to kill him because in the drug business, if somebody steals from you, and you don't kill them, the next day there'll be five other drug dealers knocking at your door saying, "Where are my drugs and money, too?"

At the same time, people were coming up to me, witnessing to me, and sharing about Jesus. So by the time I met my friend, I'd had several interactions where all kind of stuff happened when I could have gotten killed, and I got miraculously protected. But when my friend started talking about my needing to marry this girl I'd been chasing to have sex with her, I said, "I'll see you later."

Ultimately what happened was that I got food poisoning. I had smoked a joint that morning, and I made some spinach soufflé and left it on my stove in like 85-90° weather. It soured, and I came home and ate it—since I was high, as usual. The next day I woke up and I couldn't get out of bed. I called into work and said I wasn't going to come in. I had no control from either end from 8am until about 8pm. That night, I called my mother up and said, "Mom, I'm really, really sick, could you please come help me?" She cleaned me up, cleaned up the floor and bed, and took me to the hospital.

When I got into the hospital, the Holy Spirit started talking to me. As I watched other patients being wheeled next to me suffering the consequences of PCP use and other addictions, a voice said, "You know Isaiah, if you were a Christian, your life may not be perfect but you wouldn't be dealing with this, would you?" That's when I decided, I need to go to church and I need to get my life together.

So I went to the Bible study my friend had invited me to, and when the pastor shared, it was as if he were reading a book out of my life – like he knew me from the very beginning. He just knew how I felt and everything. And I accepted Jesus as my Lord and Savior that night. I really wasn't looking for God, but God was looking for me.

It was very difficult. Because of my lifestyle, I was afraid that if the people at the church found out what I had done, they'd ask me to leave. I knew if they don't want me, there's no hope. But on top of that, because I felt bad about myself, I was busy trying to earn God's love.

I would try to do stuff so that He wouldn't leave me either. I was very reticent to open up to Him, because I thought He would reject me too. It took a while of my getting to know Him better and better that I started opening up to Him.

Eventually did I open up to Him – but with fear, though. I've gone in and out of that over the course of my walk with the Lord. I have to remind myself that He actually does love me. But I was raised to perform. It took a while for me to learn that I didn't have to "perform" for God. One time the enemy was hitting me up with all these thoughts, and I realized, all the Lord had to do was stop paying attention and my world would collapse.

o   Made a Believer – Kellee

I had this pastor one time who told me that I have the spirit of doubting Thomas – that "I have to see it to believe it." I loved my father, even though he wasn't there, but it took me a while to really believe in God's love for me.

My mom really didn't start going to church every Sunday until I was a teenager. So the only time I really went to church was before my dad got locked up and a couple of times when I went to my grandmother's house. So I knew what church was, but my dad wasn't around, and my mom really wasn't into it like that. So even when she started going I was like, "Ok. That's nice." Then when it was time to move to Virginia, she just said, "I just feel like God is calling me to Virginia." My response was, "Well, He was talking to you; He ain't said nothing to me." So I came to Virginia, but I really didn't want to be here. I stayed for a couple of months, and then I wound up going back to New York trying to make it on my own.

Then I met some guy and I moved in with him and his dad. It was their house, but we were all shacked up in the basement because he was renting out to a family upstairs. That was insane. All he did was smoke and drink. I stayed there a couple of months. Then after a couple of Christmases and holidays I didn't have with my mom, I started missing her. Then I decided: "I gotta' get out of here."

This guy's Mom was dead, and they had her ashes in an urn on a bookcase. They were always supposed to spread her ashes over Virginia but they never did. I remember sleeping in the bed one night and he was sleeping really hard and I just felt something. I woke up and I saw this shadow kinda' run across the wall. I was like, "What the heck?" I was freaking out because I knew I wasn't crazy.

So I woke him up and he said, "Oh don't be afraid. That's just Ma. She likes to come and visit sometimes."

I was like, "Aww, heck no!" That thing shook me up pretty badly; I only stayed for a little while longer after that. I decided, "I have to get outta' here soon!" So I said, "Mom, I'm coming back."

Shortly after moving back to Richmond, Virginia, I met Matthew. I went to his home church. So I was at church—it was me, him, and my mom. And I'm sitting there. They were doing an altar call as normal church people do. I was sitting there minding my business and all of a sudden the minister says, "I'm going to ask a question: Do you want to receive salvation today?" or whatever. And I didn't plan on it. But all of a sudden my hand was up in the air, and I was thinking "What's going on?" I had my eyes closed, and I could feel my hand up, but I was sitting there questioning myself like, "Why is my hand up?" So that's when I got saved.

We went to that church for a little while. And then we went to another church for a while. And then we switched from that church, and now we're at ReJOYce.

After talking to both my mom and Matthew, I found out that they had both been praying vigilantly for me to receive the Lord.

I still battle with myself and try not to let the devil steal my joy by trying to tell me that I'm something that I'm not. Like when we're praising, I may look around and see people doing something and then the enemy will tell me, "If you're not doing this you really don't love God."

Even now that I know the Lord, it's still not easy at all for me to relate to God as a Father. One main reason is because I can't see Him. He's not physical and I think it's hard for me to really tap into anything that I can't actually see and touch. It's really hard to whole-heartedly love God the way I love my husband who I can see and touch. But I'm constantly trying to push past myself and continue in the fear of the Lord.

o From Brutality to Brokenness – Mike O'Coffey

My dad was kind, but he was also brutal. When I was young there's a brutality that my dad taught me that I actually never engaged in, but yet, it has helped me to know I can engage in it. It's a weird thing. I don't know if it's a guy thing, but I was glad to have gotten it. The primary reason I went into police work was to help me understand my dad better. I also thought, I'd done group home work for two years, met Selina, I wanted to marry her and I needed to make better money and police work paid better money than group home work. But mainly I thought, if I'm going to understand my dad better, I need to go to war or I have to live on the streets or I can become a police officer in an inner city. I said to myself, "Let me see how I do with all my training, with kinda' war-like pressures, and see if I do any better than my dad."

Within a year as a cop, I realized that my dad didn't do too badly. I was an unbeliever and I went and learned how to hate Blacks, and Hispanics, and Whites, and Asians – I hated everybody. I actually went beyond hatred and developed apathy toward people in their time of greatest need. It was kind of a self-protective mechanism. Very similar to what my dad described in Vietnam. And I thought, "My dad did all right, given that he'd only gone to the sixth grade" and that he was put under the pressures he was put under. Look at me, I'm put under less pressure and I see the state of my heart – the true Mike was coming out and it was not pretty.

That was ultimately what the Lord used to break me of a belief that I was okay. Yeah, because I was a straight 'A' student, student body president, valedictorian, went to Stanford, over-achieved in order to bring that honor to the family that my dad didn't bring, I darn near had an ulcer. I was bulimic my freshman year of college. There was just a lot of stress to perform, perform, perform. And when I went into police work, the ugliness of police work and what it brought out in me, made me realize I was a drowning man. I really didn't have anything to stand on within myself. There was no righteousness in me; I needed a righteousness outside of myself.

In the beginning of my third year of police work, I accepted a challenge from my dad to read the Bible. [When I had graduated from college and worked in the group home, my mom had been saved through watching some televangelist. She had a Bible and she just felt like she needed to read the Bible – boy she went at it with a vengeance! She proclaimed faith in Christ and my dad soon after.] Then they just kept trying to give me Bible after Bible.

After I got married, they gave me and Selina Bible after Bible. And I kept telling them, "You guys gotta' stop giving me Bibles. You're insulting my Jewish wife. And don't you know this is just the opiate of the masses – like Nietzsche said, 'it soothes the conscience of the weak to believe that the strong will some day pay'."

I thought I was so smart, but I was just an idiot. That's how I would disrespect my parents, but they were patient. Dad was also blunt. He pulled me to the side one day and said, "You ever read that Bible?"

And I said, "C'mon Dad, you guys sent me to Catholic school. Remember? I had an Old Testament semester and I had a New Testament semester."

It takes a dad to do something like this, he goes, "No, hot shot! I mean have you ever read it cover to cover – so that if someone told you it said something you would know whether it said it or not?" Oh yeah, he added, "Like those other thousands of books you've read cover-to-cover" – like, "you little snot."

And I was like, "Well, no."

And he goes, "So what's stoppin' ya'?"

So I said, "I don't know." So he kinda' trapped me. First time I'd gotten trapped by my dad. 'Cause he'd gotten kinda' upset with my attitude, which is the right thing for a dad to do.

This was right after two years at OPD. So I started reading my Bible. A couple of friends of mine had been killed already. So I had started to think more about life and death kinda' stuff. And what if this Bible's right? And I did see a change in my dad.

I remember one day after a very hard midnight shift. I was sitting on the hallway in Alameda in a house we had there. There'd been multiple shootings the night before and a friend of mine had been killed only a week earlier in a car stop (he got out and the guy had an AK-47 and just lit him up); another friend of mine had responded code 3, a car pulled out, and he had to take out three parked cars, he pulverized his right knee and broke his pelvis in three places and couldn't be a cop again. So that morning I was reading through John, and I got to 16:24. John 16:24 says, "Until now, you have not asked for anything in My Name. Ask and you will receive and your joy will be complete." I remember screaming out to the Lord, "Oh yeah?! Okay, Jesus, so I'm asking in your name, what am I supposed to do?" And IMMEDIATELY the phone rang. It was a guy who just was an acquaintance.

He says, "Hey Mike. It's Steve Von Ehrenkrook and I'm calling you to let you know there's a men's retreat and it's going to be in a couple of weeks and I just wanted to know if you were going to go?"

I said, "No way."

He says, "What do you mean no way?"

I go, "That's not why you're calling."

He goes, "Yeah it is. Why are you saying that?"

I say, "Listen to what I just read."

And I read it to him and he goes, "Well, I guess you got your answer!"

It happened to be at the same time as this man-centered, we're just going to "pull ourselves up by our bootstraps and be men" Justin Sterling retreat that I was considering. You can see I was questioning "how do I be a man?" It was the cry of my heart. And what do I do to just be a man? It's kind of a hard thing to know, especially since we've got such a feminized society. Now I was driving fast, *pulling guns out, and arresting guys, and beating on people – is that what a man is? Do I need to take care of my wife better? All this other kinda' stuff. So I was reading here where Jesus says how your joy can be complete – could it be?*

After a series of events indicative of the war over our souls, I did go to that Christian retreat with Steve and, boy, God broke me. And it was through the story, by the way, of another father. I still remember where I was sitting in the pews when I realized how much I wanted this Christ this father was talking about. The story he told was of the forgiveness of God the Father, which I wanted so much. Tim, himself, had very dark hair. He said when he was in college he got his girlfriend – a red-headed girl – pregnant. He convinced her to get an abortion. Many years later, he married another brunette. And they had a son who had bright red hair. Tim said when he saw the red hair, it was like the mercy of God telling him, "Though you killed one, I'm giving you another." So here was another man trying to figure out what it means to be a father and needing Christ to help him. That broke me. That's when I realized that the God of the Bible is worth following.

*So from that point on—that was June of 1995—my life's **never** been the same! It has been a pretty clear pursuit of deeper and deeper levels of the presence of God in my life. That is ultimately what I want and that is the inheritance I have to give to my children.*

A CALL TO WHOLENESS

"There is no pit too deep where God is not deeper still."
– Corrie Ten Boom, "The Hiding Place"

Food on the table and a roof over one's head is nice but nothing makes up for a loving, nurturing relationship with one's father. While not having a father would make it more difficult, it doesn't make it impossible to bond with a child. Bonding is more of an innate need or spiritual drive, than simply a learned behavior. Therefore, fatherless fathers are not doomed to repeat their own childhood experiences.[1]

My father is a great example. His father was definitely NOT the nurturing type. His primary method of encouragement was "bullying." And while he taught my dad a lot of things, they were hardly godly. So for the first many years of his teenage and young adult life, my father emulated his father's womanizing ways and lascivious lifestyle. I am pleased and proud that after meeting God, for the rest of his life, he steadily grew into the father after God's own heart that he wanted to be. Was he flawless? Absolutely not. But the transformations God wrought in his heart were experienced by his children who chose to forgive his shortcomings and allow him to be their father. "Forgiveness liberates the soul. That's why it's such a powerful weapon."[2]

Jesus speaks of the Father's love as the ultimate blessing to humanity when He prays in John 17:23: "That the world may know that You . . . have loved them, even as You have loved Me." One of the most poignant depictions I've seen of the depth of the Father's love for the Son – and therefore for me – is the scene in *The Passion of the Christ* right after Jesus commends His spirit to the Father. That single, solitary tear which falls from heaven is so full of the fire of His passion and the agony of that first and momentary separation from the Son that it causes the earth to quake, Roman centurions to surrender on bent knees, and the veil secluding the Holiest Place in the temple to be rent from top to bottom.

But you can't give what you don't have. "If you don't see yourself as being loved, you're going to have a hard time loving." We love Him because He first loved us. [I John 4:19] That's why some of you have low self-esteem or identity problems because you don't know the unconditional love that God has for you. When you know God loves you, everyone else in your life can act crazy if they want to, but you know the "Main Man" loves you![3]

Although children are not held responsible for the sins of their parents, they are definitely affected and negatively impacted by them. There is no such thing as perfect earthly fathers, but because of the spiritual authority and influential role they play in our lives, they have shaped who we are, what we experience, what we believe, and what direction we've taken as we've grown up. We will tend to be predisposed to living in their wake, making their same mistakes, believing the same lies, and maybe even struggling with the same issues and addictions. And the "generations of a family will lead one another further and further away from God unless a chain breaker steps up and turns things around."[4] Will you take up the mantle?

○ Forgiveness is Key – Alex

First of all, if you're saved, then you should have a sense of forgiveness –even before-hand before meeting the father with whom you're trying to reconcile. You need to do that moreso for your personal development than for him. But it does help to give that "dad" the benefit of the doubt. At least that was true in my case. Sometimes you just don't know the whole story.

Then again, I have friends whose fathers are completely malicious to them – who would do all types of crazy things to them: steal their identity, credit card theft, take out a whole bunch of car loans and leave them in debt. I mean that's your child, you don't do that to your own child. It's kinda' hard to forgive and look past that, but I think as a child, as much as you resent that, there's always still that longing to connect. And sometimes you just have to try – even if that father's not ready to acknowledge you or even meet you. You still, at the end of the day, need to say, "I tried." And I have no regrets. Give it to God and just keep praying for that person.

o Bearing the Pain of the Past – Giji

I thought that once I'd met my father, and everything was going well with our reunion, that I'd resolved any "old" issues about his absence in my childhood—no use crying over spilled milk. Right? Not quite.

My mother and I had a tumultuous relationship from the day my brother went to the University of Miami—on my tenth birthday, in fact—and for the next 20 years. My mother had never spoken an unkind word about my father, so I saw no correlation between him and my difficult relationship with my mom. It had occurred to me that, at times, perhaps because of something I'd done or said that reminded her of my father, I may have caused a wound to be opened. But since their friendship was also rekindled in my reunion with my dad, I really didn't see any reason to consider my father's absence as a source of my contention with my mother, either.

Then, after walking with the Lord pretty solidly for about 10 years, I participated in the longest and most painful pastoral counseling appointment I've had to this day. It started out with a request to meet with my assistant pastor to work through internal conflicts I was having in her and my relationship. She often said things that pressed the same nerves my mom did and, on the inside, I'd have the same reaction. Because I understood the importance of being in right relationship with my leadership, as a lay leader in my church, I earnestly wanted to work this out.

We started talking at about 10pm. And we talked. And we talked. When Pastor finally kicked us out of the pastoral suite at 4am, so he could go to bed, Vonda and I moved our session to the living room and talked a little bit more. Sensing that there was something, yet, to be broken, which neither of us had been able to identify, Vonda began praying over me and told me to just pray in the Spirit until something came up in my spirit. Whatever it was, even if it didn't seem related, she said I should just renounce it.

Suddenly, I became aware that I was still very angry with my mother, and at some level mad at God, for their allowing me to grow up without my father. My mother was the one who'd walked away and had decided there would be no contact. Then the dam broke. I cried so hard and so long that I honestly thought at one point I might have a heart attack. My body was heaving so violently as I cried that, while Vonda held me, trying to comfort me as she continued to pray over me, I inadvertently pulled her and me off the couch and onto the floor. Anguish so deep, I had buried even the memory of the pain. When the last tear was shed, and my breathing had returned to normal, and forgiveness had been wrestled from the depths of my soul, the sun was coming up, and I had a new appreciation for Isaiah 61:3 in the beauty He'd given me for ashes.

o   From Crayons to Perfume – Fran

As a female, I can say with certainty that men and women get different things from their fathers. As a woman, our relationship with our father either helps us to be secure and confident as women or it causes us to feel uncovered. And I really felt uncovered. These words I didn't really know at the beginning of everything, but it's what the Lord showed me. I didn't realize how insecure I was because I didn't have a father to affirm me when I was younger. My first impression was that my father only calls me when he's drunk or been drinking. I just thought he doesn't think about me unless he's drinking. So basically my view of a father was not one of love, not one of someone I go to in order to get my affirmation; this is somebody who I felt antagonized me.

In reconciling both my relationship with the Lord and with my father, the Lord started showing me He needed to heal some things from the earthly father relationship before I could operate in, enjoy, or totally benefit from the Heavenly Father relationship. And I'm a much more secure woman now – much more affirmed by getting to know God as Father and having gone through the healing process as a result of not having received that affirmation and covering from an earthly father.

o   Don't Wait Until It's Too Late – Felecia

I believe that it's very important to say and do the things that are important and forgive while our people are still here, as opposed to waiting until they're at death's door or they've passed on you don't have that closure that you needed. We will have to answer for that. So I'm thankful that my father and I had the connection and that we had the bond at some point in my adult life so that I could say with a clean heart the father-daughter bond was there, the grandfather-grandchildren bond was there, and I know that if he were still here, he would love and adore his great-grandchildren.

So I'm thankful for what we did have. And, no, it didn't play out in a lifetime, but, by the same token, what other way would God have had it to prepare me to be able to sit here today for this story . . . for such a time as this. [Esther 4:14] He has allowed me to see we have to have some connection with the biological earthly father and know his voice, so that when the Heavenly Father speaks, we can abide in what He says and know His voice to be obedient. And that is so key and critical as to why so many people, including Christians, don't know what God sounds like. It's because they haven't heard the biological father; they don't have the proper connection.

o Jesus Loves Me, This I Know – Isaiah

The Heavenly Father got involved in my relationship with my earthly father and caused it to be restored. That's my only real testimony. I just had enough sense to pray. It wasn't anything I did; the Holy Spirit choreographed it all on His own.

What the Lord has done is that He has demonstrated over and over again how much He loves me. And it's often the little things He'll do, and sometimes the big things. But I'm starting to gain a confidence in His love, and that His love is perfect. And He really does understand me, and He really does care about how I feel. There's things He wants to do with my life that supersede some of my own passions—my own desires, which I understand—but He really does love me. The Bible says He understood my thoughts from afar off. [Psalm 139:2] And it's true.

But it's still a work in progress, where I'll go back to performing again. I'll say, "Okay, I didn't hit all the notes today so He must be mad." And realize, "No, if you made a mistake, that's what the blood is for." Even if you did something intentionally, the blood of Jesus is strong enough to wash that away. So what's been happening is that He really has been wooing me back to Himself, to understand what a father's love really is.

o No Regrets – Giji & Bobby Deadwyler

I can hardly believe that it has been over thirty years since I first "met" my father. Perhaps it is because of the incredible torrent of emotions I felt then that it seems like a much shorter season. Or, perhaps it's because I've played back the events over and over again on my mind's viewfinder that the memories have not even begun to wane. For me, this tremendous experience of reunion began the night before my graduation from high school and climaxed in a visit from my father on July 7, 1979. For my father, the quest had begun 16 years prior and voiced its last temporal expression in September of 1997. For both of us, this sojourn will find its rest in eternity . . . . In fact, God had a plan from the foundations of the earth whereby we would be together forever.

So as you see, Daddy and I were kinda' "doubly" cut from the same piece of cloth. That's a major part of the beauty of all of this–my father and I will have an eternity to spend with each other and our Heavenly Father. While there is nothing that could be done to "make-up" for the time that we were unable to spend together for the first seventeen-and-a-half years of my life, we have a connection that transcends all time and space which continually enriched the relationship Daddy and I shared for eighteen years, until his Homegoing on November 2, 1997.

Do I have any regrets about having not grown up with my father? Do I feel robbed? I have in the past. Understanding that I have a Heavenly Father–Who has known the end from the beginning for each of our lives, Who had both my and Daddy's best interests at heart in everything He allowed, and Who worked all things together for my and his good because we love Him and are called according to His purposes– has made forgetting those things which lay behind and pressing on to what lies ahead much easier. And my father expressed similar sentiments.

I adore you beyond words of expression. I've stopped wasting meaningless time wishing my knees could have been available for your growing yester-years to sit on, and accept the reality of the fact that Kha did not grant me that opportunity. But ever since that privilege presented itself, I immediately rushed into your life! The love of the Lord's blessing had given me another step of joy to rise upon! I happen to be in love with God and also with you, the daughter He blessed me with!

Don't get me wrong, when I got the call from my brother, Ross, telling me that our father had died, I had to seriously fight feelings of being robbed of him . . . again—feelings of anger that I hadn't had the opportunity to say, "Goodbye," just like with Motherdear, Gramma', and Auntie Marian. Particularly because I had received a call the day before telling me my father's leg had been amputated and I didn't call him because the doctors said the surgery had been a huge success and he was out of the woods, so I thought I'd let him get some rest before I called the next afternoon, which turned out to be too late.

There have been many, many, times that I have wished for more years to share ministry opportunities with my dad, seek his advice on a variety of issues, discuss a movie we'd both seen, and take trips together to see my brother Rick and his family, like we used to. I only spent **one** Christmas with my father in my entire life, when I was about 25—and that carried the price of a huge fight with my mom.

Yet, I, too, mostly just feel blessed – blessed to have had an opportunity to know my earthly father, at all; blessed that he, too, was a Spirit-filled believer with whom I could share and from whom I could seek comfort and counsel; blessed that, although I didn't get to see him nearly as often as I'd have liked, that the Lord did open up opportunities for us to visit, including the last time just three months before his home-going; blessed that the testimony of our reunion has and will serve as an inspiration to others who seek reconciliation and restoration of broken family relationships. It's God's life and love in us which all this time, even when we were apart, has made us inseparable.

○ Where's My Story?

➢ My father died in the war when I was six – I barely even remember him and I never had any surrogates . . .
➢ I was physically and emotionally abused by my father for years – I've been going to therapy, but I'm still pretty angry…
➢ My father is alive, knows I'm alive, but refuses to acknowledge me or have any contact with me – I'm 35 years old and I've never even met the man…
➢ I got a girl pregnant in college. I told her to have an abortion and when she refused, I told her it was her choice to deal with the consequences. I've never met or taken any responsibility for my child…
➢ I was repeatedly raped by my father as a teenager and no one came to my rescue; he made me get an abortion when I got pregnant with his child…
➢ My father sold me into child pornography when I was six years old, and then abandoned me when his pedophiliac friends stopped being interested when I was 13 and started developing; I think he's still in prison for molesting somebody else's kid…

> ➢ My father died when I was a young adult, but we never got a chance to reconcile our differences – I hadn't even spoken to the man in 10 years…
> ➢ I introduced my son to drugs, alcohol, and sex when he was 11 years old. I've since come to the Lord, but my son's a drug-addicted drag queen in a gay bar…
> ➢ My alcoholic step-mother used to cut me with broken vodka bottles, burn me with cigarette butts, and beat my knuckles until they bled, while my father watched TV, ignoring my screams coming from the bathroom or the bedroom – I ran away at 14 and haven't seen either of them since…

Those of us who did share our stories may not be able to relate to exactly what you've gone through, but Jesus can. The Bible says that He was touched with the feelings of all our infirmities and temptations, yet without sin [Heb. 4:15] – a man of sorrows, acquainted with grief [Isaiah 53:3]. You can be assured that the afflictions you have experienced as a result of abusive or inadequate fathering are, indeed, working an eternal weight of glory on your behalf. [2 Cor. 4:17] Jesus came to heal the broken-hearted and to bind up their wounds [Psalm 147:3] . . . no matter how deep.

We are not so naïve as to think that there is a magic wand of forgiveness and healing that you can wave, and all will be well. In some cases, your unresolved conflict has gone to the grave of your child or father. You may have to finish your part of the dance like Adam did, or go to the gravesite and speak aloud to release someone like Nathan did, in the movie "Courageous."

In some cases, you may have no idea of the location of the father or child removed from your life. You might be fortunate enough to reconnect eventually like David did with his little girl in "Courageous," but for some of you the ending will not be so happy. A father or a child may still refuse to acknowledge you or you may never locate them. That is when it becomes all the more imperative to fully engage in the relationship the Heavenly Father offers you. He is the only one who can fill those voids in your soul. Even if your mother and father have forsaken you, the Lord promises to take care of you. [Psalm 27:10]

If you were the abused or an abuser in the relationship, for any length of time, you may need professional counseling, deliverance prayer, group therapy, or some combination of the above. Remember that there is safety in a multitude of godly counsel. [Prov. 11:14]

Do what you need to do to get free and be able to walk in the wholeness Jesus died to purchase for you. Don't let His tremendous sacrifice be in vain in your life. But it's not just going to fall down from the sky like a mantle over you. You will have to pursue it and pay the price to win. For this healing and satisfied father hunger are, certainly, parts of the prize to which the high calling of God in Christ Jesus is pressing every believer upward. [Phil. 3:14]

o   A Word for the Wounded Children

Forgiveness means that you've put away what they've done and cast it into the sea of your forgetfulness, just like God did. But if you still feel some kind of pain, some kind of anger, some kind of resentment, come up in you when you think about him, you haven't really forgiven him. Real forgiveness is when you are able to pray for him from your heart with joy.

The forgiveness you choose toward your father is a key that will unlock your relationship to others. You will never overcome and become the man or woman of God you want to be if you don't forgive your daddy.

No one is disregarding or invalidating the pain you suffered due to your father's inadequacies, but that's yesterday. The Word of God says you are a new creature. What you're dealing with now are your memory banks. In reality, all those things are already healed inside of you; you just have to choose to walk in it.[5]

Ralph Keyes offers seven suggestions for sons who want to reach out to their fathers, but I think they apply for daughters, as well: 1) Take the initiative to start the conversation. 2) Don't begin the conversation with grievances, no matter how justified. 3) Listen to what your father has to say; don't butt in, argue, or mentally compose a response while he's talking. 4) Search for common ground. Are you experiencing some of the same things he went through? Do you have fond memories of time you spent together? Say so. 5) Keep in mind that your father is also a son, too. 6) Remember that it's as important for your father to hear that you care for him as it is for you to hear it from your dad. 7) Tell him soon. Next year may be too late – or next week, or even tomorrow.[6]

Ultimately, the goal is to embrace the full inheritance God offers you as your Heavenly Father, regardless of the outcome with your earthly father. There are no age requirements. Amanda Geesey, at 17, came to the understanding of how God could help her navigate through her feelings of abandonment, hurt and distrust of men. You can do the same. God is not a respecter of persons. [Acts 10:34] God will prove Himself faithful as a loving, forgiving, and caring Father. He will show you that not only are you safe under the shadow of His wings, but that your name is willingly engraved on the palm of His hand [Isaiah 49:16] and you will never be forgotten.[7]

o A Word for the Struggling Fathers

The fathers of this generation need to realize that they are important and that they can make a big difference in their kids' lives, whether they live or die, and how they go about doing so.

As you embark on this journey, "You will need to allow time and effort for grieving, healing, and restoring your heart. Once your heart has been 'reconditioned,' you can move forward.[8]

If you want to be the kind of father God's ordained you to be, the bottom line is, like David, being "a man after God's own heart." In that way, you can become a father after God's own heart. Only then can you model the Father's heart to your children – by reflecting holiness and purity, by showing yourself to be truthful and trustworthy, by being a comfort and a refuge to your children. In the midst of your "becoming," be careful not to lose sight of the Lord's commitment to "participate" in every aspect of your life. Only His Spirit can create the qualities and skills you need to become a father after His heart. Your part is to walk with Him through the fathering experience, daily inviting and anticipating His active, faithful involvement.[9]

You have to decide to look away from your investment portfolio, step out of your office or off the golf course, turn off ESPN, or get your head out from under the hood of your car long enough "to ruminate over the mystery of a father's love for his daughter and a daughter's love for her father." Dr. Leman believes "a good percentage of a man's ultimate happiness, meaning, and fulfillment lie in that relationship."[10]

Even your "best plans can go awry, because sheer determination isn't enough." . . . But you can join the army of 'ordinary' fathers who are "connecting with thousands of other fathers who are simply committed to being the best dads [you] can be." You no longer have to allow your pasts, nor your current pursuits or aspirations, keep you from developing a deep, abiding relationship with your children. Your children deserve much more than "the leftovers of your energies and emotions. . . . What it requires on your part is a commitment of the heart."[11]

Will you be one of the men who, "regardless of the mistakes [you've] made in the past, regardless of what [y]our father did or did not do for [you], will give the strength of [y]our arms and the rest of [y]our days to loving God with all that [you] are and teach [y]our children to do the same[?]"[12]

*   *   *   *   *

There is a story in the Talmud about a king who had a son who had gone astray from his father. The son was told, "Return to your father." The son said, "I cannot." His father sent a messenger to say, "Return as far as you can and I will come to you the rest of the way."[13]

I want to encourage every child and every father with unresolved issues in their father-child relationship(s) to "break free from [y]our family weaknesses by the power of God – by seeking Him, trusting Him, and following Him instead"—returning as far as you can.[14] God wants to do a healing in the hearts of His people. His grace will meet you where you are and be sufficient to see you through. [2 Cor. 12:9]

ENDNOTES

Chapter 1 - The Cry of Father Hunger

1. H.B. Biller & R.J. Trotter, *The Father Factor, (New York: Simon & Schuster, 1994)*.
2. Carey Roberts, "Yes, Fathers Are Essential," LewRockwell.com, 2004.
3. Robert Huxley, LMFT, "The Importance of the Father/Child Bond," ParentingToolbox.com.
4. Ken Canfield, Ph.D., *The Heart of a Father*, (Chicago: Northfield Publishing, 1996), 13.
5. Assistant Pastor Vonda Pipkin, "Knowing the Father's Love," Sermon. Delivered at a Women's Aglow Conference, Richmond, VA, October 7, 1995.
6. Trace L. Hansen, Ph.D., "Love Isn't Enough," www.ruthinstitute. org/articles, MercatorNet.com, June 2, 2009.
7. Stephen & Alex Kendrick, *The Resolution for Men*, (Nashville: B&H Publishing Group, 2011), 20.
8. Rexanne Mancini, "The Importance of Fathers," www.rexanne. com, (2000-2004).
9. Kendrick, *The Resolution for Men*, 20.
10. Mancini, "The Importance of Fathers."
11. Dr. Kevin Leman, *What a Difference a Daddy Makes*, (Nashville: Thomas Nelson, 2000), 5, 11.
12. Mancini, "The Importance of Fathers."
13. Ralph Keyes, "Father Figure," *Chicago Tribune Magazine*, June 21, 1992, 10.

Chapter 2 - Genesis

1. Canfield, *The Heart of a Father*, 19.
2. Ralph Keyes, "If Only I Could Say, 'I Love You, Dad'," *Parade Magazine*, February 7, 1993, 4.

Chapter 6 – Pivotal Pillars

1. Pastor Chester C. Pipkin, Jr., "Restoring the Children Back to Their Fathers," Sermon. Delivered at ReJOYce In Jesus Ministries, Los Angeles, CA, June 19, 2004.
2. Canfield, *The Heart of a Father*, 19.
3. Canfield, *The Heart of a Father*, 88. For more insight, see "The I CANs" profiles developed by the National Center for Fathering.

Chapter 7 – Voice of the Father

1. Pipkin, "Restoring the Children."
2. Amanda Lynn Geesey, "The Importance of the Father in the Home," The Center for Parent/Youth Understanding, 2004.
3. Geesey, "The Importance of a Father in the Home."
4. Josh McDowell, *The Father Connection*, (Nashville: B&H Publishing Group, 1996), 16-17.
5. Kendrick, *The Resolution for Men*, 104-105.
6. Josh McDowell, "The Vital Role of Fathering," audio message, Focus on the Family Radio Broadcast Ministry, 2005.
7. Geesey, "The Importance of a Father in the Home."
8. James I. Schaller, *The Search for Lost Fathering*, (Grand Rapids: Revell, 1995).
9. Norman H. Wright, *Always Daddy's Little Girl*, (Ventura: Division of Gospel Light, 2001).
10. Shawn Donovan, "The Importance of Fatherhood."
11. Geesey, "The Importance of a Father in the Home."
12. Kendrick, *The Resolution for Men*, 229-30.
13. Pipkin, "Restoring the Children."
14. McDowell, *The Father Connection*, 14.
15. Kendrick, *The Resolution for Men*, 249.
16. Seth Metcalf, "The Importance of Father's Time," FatherMag.com, 2002.
17. Roberts, "Yes Fathers Are Essential."
18. Canfield, *The Heart of a Father*, 14.

Chapter 8 – Second Chapters of Life

1. Pipkin, "Restoring the Children."

Chapter 10 – The Eternal Context

1. Ken Gire, *Moments With the Savior*, (Grand Rapids: Zondervan, 1998), 245.
2. Ibid, 246.
3. Pipkin, "Knowing the Father's Love."
4. McDowell, *The Father Connection*, 18.
5. McDowell, *The Father Connection*, 19.
6. Leman, *What a Difference*, 156.
7. Ibid, 157, 166.
8. Ibid, 159.
9. Ibid, 161.

Chapter 11 – A Call to Wholeness

1. Ron Huxley, LMFT, "The Importance of the Father/Child Bond," ParentingToolbox.com.
2. South African President Nelson Mandela in "Invictus," Warner Bros. Entertainment, Inc., 2009.
3. Pipkin, "Knowing the Father's Love."
4. Kendrick, *The Resolution for Men*, 40.
5. Pipkin, "Restoration of the Children."
6. Keyes, "If Only I Could Say, 'I Love You, Dad',"5.
7. Geesey, "The Importance of a Father in the Home."
8. Canfield, *The Heart of a Father*, 13.
9. McDowell, *The Father Connection*, 166, 168.
10. Leman, *What a Difference*, 18, 22.
11. Canfield, *The Heart of a Father*, 11, 257.
12. Kendrick, *The Resolution for Men*, 249.
13. The narrator in "The Chosen," The Chosen Film Company, 1981.
14. Kendrick, *The Resolution for Men*, 40.

ACKNOWLEDGMENTS

All glory to God in Heaven who scripted my purpose, my Messiah and King, Yeshua who's purchased my life and whose Word is my light and salvation, and the precious Holy Spirit, who truly is the Author and Finisher of this work. I am honored and grateful to have been chosen to be a co-laborer in fulfilling this assignment.

A special thanks to all those named and unnamed who were willing to earnestly share their own father-child relationships as a ministry of reconciliation to others. I certainly could not have written this without you.

To my wonderful editorial team – Marita Robbins, Renée Canada, Renét Dennard-Cole (*a.k.a. Cousin Penny*), and Edith Okai—for lending your individual giftings, as well as your collective enthusiasm and encouragement, in getting this manuscript publisher-ready. You were the faithful mid-wives in the birth of this project.

A thousand thanks to Dr. Ken Canfield, not only for the wonderful endorsement, but for the probing questions you asked prior to making that commitment, which significantly impacted the practical development of the book.

They say "good things come to those who wait," and I am so glad that I was able to wait and receive a stamp of approval from the National Center for Fathering. Many thanks, Mr. Casey, for adding the review of my manuscript for endorsement to your already very full plate.

To my Angel Investors– Yolanda McCoy, Coretta Mincey Monts, Edith Lewis, Stefanie Belnavis, George and Sonya Ramsey, Kesha Weekes, and those who wish to remain anonymous– I offer my deepest gratitude. While there were dollar figures attached to your giving, your friendship and support are immeasurable. Chioma, may you be blessed a hundred-fold for your generosity. I truly believe that the seed you sowed a few years ago will reap a harvest in the full manifestation of the projects the Lord has placed in you to dispense.

Many thanks to my Dennard family and all the brothers and sisters in my ReJOYce family who have joined their faith together with mine to provide over a decade of moral support and prayer cover to see this book finally in print.

And last, but certainly not least, my heartfelt gratitude to Brian Fox, Sarah Goddard, Jason Klarke, Michael Eckhardt, and the rest of the CrossBooks publishing staff who were the wind beneath my wings in delivering *Hungry for Wholeness* to the marketplace.

About the Author:

Giji Mischel Dennard, born in St. Petersburg, Florida, is a graduate of Howard University (B.A., Print Journalism) and Stanford Law School (J.D.). She has been an avid reader, with a preference for non-fiction, since grade school. As writer, artist, and chef, amid the process of starting her own catering and event planning business in northern California, Giji wrote, designed, and self-published a 151-recipe cookbook entitled *Feasts Fit for a King: Food for the Body & Soul*, which includes practical kitchen tips and biblical wisdom on Kingdom living.

Hungry for Wholeness is her second publication, thanks to the support of CrossBooks Publishing. Giji has been a lay leader in college student ministry with ReJOYce in Jesus Campus Fellowship on the East and West Coasts for the last 20 years. She currently resides in Montgomery County, Maryland, and recently began working full-time for the owner of an automobile dealership, handling project management, marketing development and coordination, strategic planning analysis, event planning, and website administration.

CPSIA information can be obtained at www.ICGtesting.com
Printed in the USA
BVOW010143061112

304691BV00001B/7/P